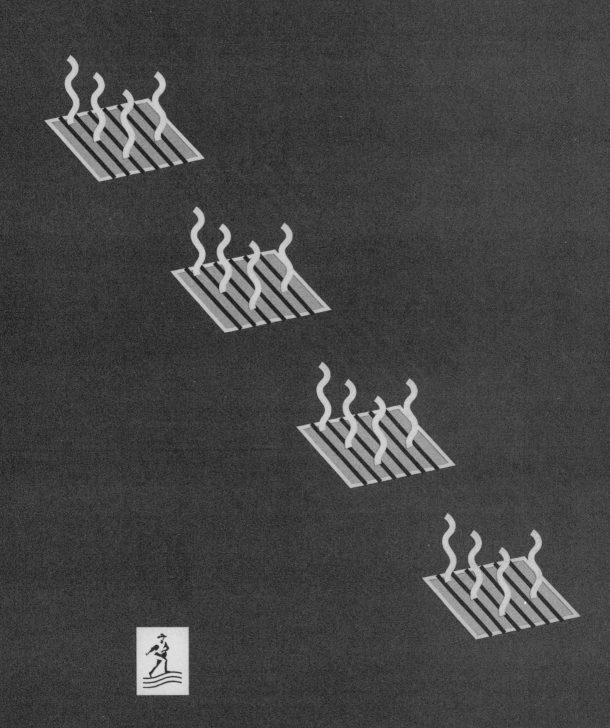

by george foreman and joel engel

By George:
The Autobiography
of George Foreman

by george foreman and cherie calbom

George Foreman's
Knock-Out-the-Fat
Barbecue and Grilling Cookbook

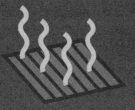

More Than 75 Recipes for Family and Friends

George Foreman and Barbara Witt

Simon & Schuster
new york · london
toronto · sydney
singapore

George Foreman's Big Book of Grilling, Barbecue, and Rotisserie

SIMON & SCHUSTER
Rockefeller Center
1230 Avenue of the Americas
New York, NY 10020

BOOK DESIGN BY DEBORAH KERNER
"GRILL" ART BY RICHARD WAXBERG

Manufactured in the United States of America

10   9   8   7   6   5   4   3   2   1

Library of Congress Cataloging-in-Publication Data

Foreman, George
    George Foreman's big book of grilling, barbecue, and rotisserie : more than 75 recipes
for family and friends / George Foreman and Barbara Witt.
        p. cm.
    1. Barbecue cookery.   I. Witt, Barbara.   II. Title.

TX840.B3 F65 2000
641.5'784—dc21   00-057385

ISBN 0-7432-0092-6

This book is dedicated to

Willie, Mary, and Gloria Ann,

my beloved sisters,

who from day to day attend to all my cooking needs

with a touch of Mother's love.

And to

Hermite Martelly,

my mother-in-law,

who keeps the Caribbean spices coming.

Acknowledgments

MY THANKS GO TO BARBARA WITT,
THE BEST CORNER PERSON AN EX-BOXER COULD EVER HAVE;

TO MARIAN ALTSHULER,
WHO IS THE GET-IT-DONE CHAMP;

TO HENRY HOLMES,
WITHOUT WHOM THERE
IS NO WAY TO KEEP A CLEAR HEAD TO COOK;

AND TO THE FOLKS AT SALTON FOR STAYING CLOSE.

AND TO ALL THE GEORGE FOREMAN FANS
WHO REALLY MADE ME AND GAVE ME THE SMILE.

—GEORGE FOREMAN

Contents

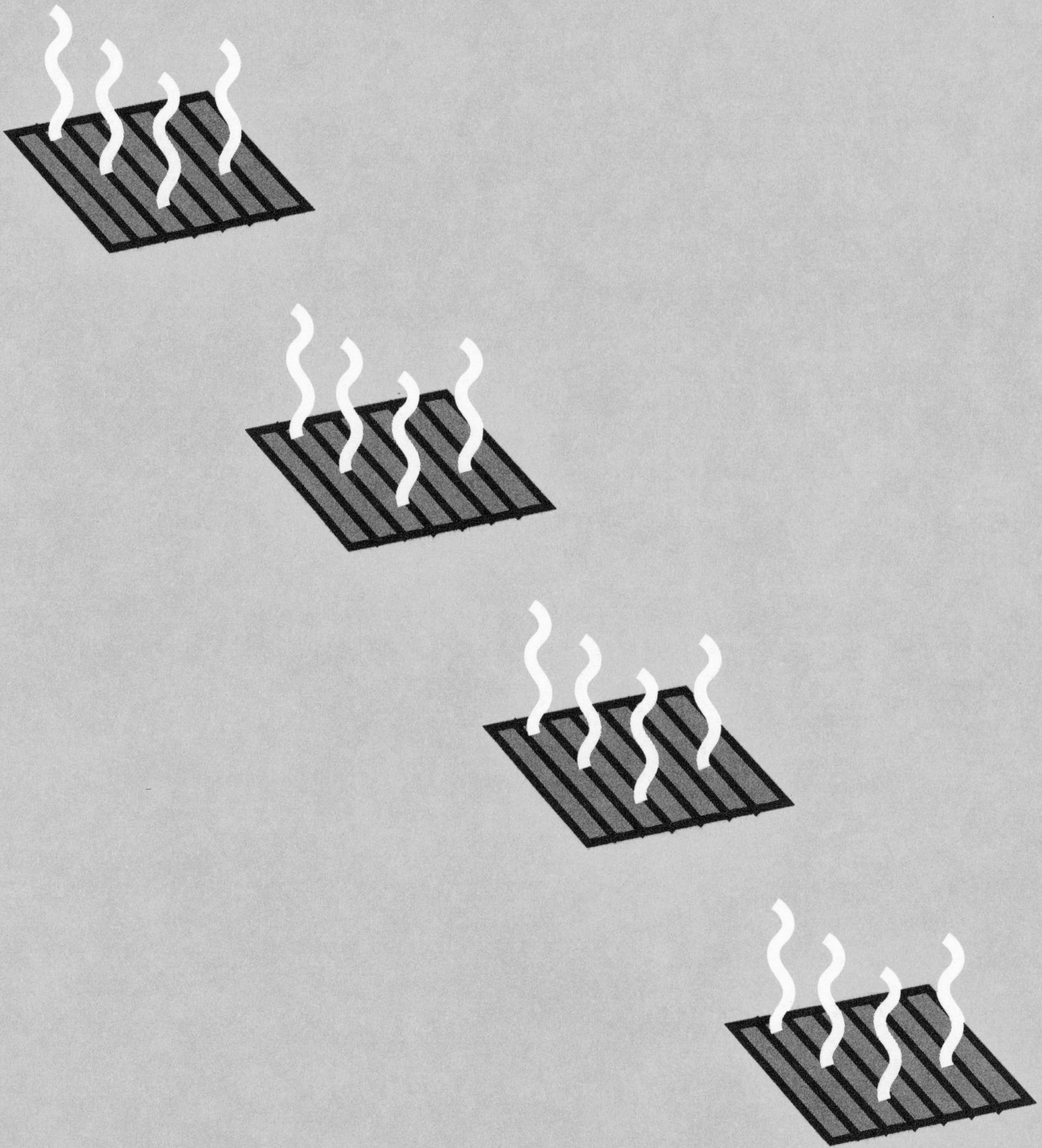

Foreword

What better way to celebrate a new millennium, a new century, and a new year than to revisit historic barbecuing and grilling in its modern forms? These recipes capture the diverse flavor memories of my travels, allowing me to savor them all over again along with the good times that made me say, "I am alive—I have made it—I am happy."

In 1967 I took my first trip abroad to Germany. Then there was my Olympic Gold Medal win in Mexico City. What a happy time it was for me when I walked around the ring with my American flag, making sure the whole world knew I was an American. Three and a half years later, in Kingston, Jamaica, the world once again saw that same American jump for joy when Howard Cosell yelled over and over, "Down goes Frasier! Down goes Frasier!" As World Heavyweight Champion, I soon went to Tokyo to defend my title, then faced challenger Kim Norton in Caracas, Venezuela, and finally the famous "Rumble in the Jungle" against the great Muhammad Ali. Although both joy and disappointment were with me on my journey, something more lasting remains. The world opened its doors, its heart, and the hospitality of its table to me. I was treated to the best food I could ever have imagined. When soups and appetizers were served, I said to myself, "I hope I like this." Even vegetables and breads were big "maybes" for me. But when the open-air grilling or barbecuing started, we all became one. These wonderful places were new to me, and the exotic seasonings and aromas made me realize I was truly the world champ. In this cookbook you will travel with me and revisit Europe, Mexico, the Caribbean, Africa, Latin America, and finally home to America. I hope you, too, will feel some of my joy and wonder in having been the Heavyweight Champion of the World.

George Foreman

Introduction

It's been a winding, scented trail of barbecue drippings from the pits of the Arawak Indians and marauding pirates on the beaches of Haiti, around the compass of North America, and well beyond. The Caribs called the green branch rack that hung the roasting pig over animal-bone briquettes a *bocan.* The French named it *boucan,* and the Spanish *barbacoa.* From those rowdy beach parties came the English synonym for pirate, buccaneer, and the French verb *boucaner,* meaning to dry-smoke or cure.

So what began as a necessity for food preservation has become an abiding infatuation with the romance of the flame. Cooking and eating outdoors is at once communal and festive. Irresistible images flood quickly to mind, from happy Hollywood hobos around a twig-fired stew pot to a bunch of kids roasting weenies and marshmallows over a summer campfire. Very little can beat the draw to a chilly clambake on a New England beach or the lure of a sultry Hawaiian luau. No doubt, Native Americans originated our dinner dance—and truly, have you ever had to refuse a cook-out invitation without deep sighs of regret?

Cooking over the primal flame is all about the aroma and flavor of wood smoke, natural or carbonized. At first, the simple thrill of the grill inspired many suburban Americans to jerry-build a backyard pile of rocks and a hardware store grate into a culinary fireplace, which led to some serious and wildly fanciful mortar-and-brick extravaganzas. Then along came the minimalist, movable little Japanese hibachi, followed by our own Mr. Weber's inventive, and quickly ubiquitous, kettle grill. The southern hand-forged iron country cooker with the quaint tophat chimney—large enough to cook a haunch of anything—eventually morphed into a sleek, enameled city grill. Today the rich and famous are wheeling stainless-steel mini kitchens to their terraces with all manner of gadgetry attached.

It wasn't long before the fuss and mess of burning charcoal caused many barbecue enthusiasts to sacrifice the flavor of the smoke and switch to quick ignition by gas. Now plug-and-play electric grills have found a deep market not only with city dwellers lacking backyards or patios but also with homeowners whose busy lives have forced them to abandon the labor-intensive *barbacoa* to more leisurely occasions. The new millennium marks the quick and clean era of contemporary grilling, something restaurant chefs learned the merits of long ago.

So what's so great about those perfect brown stripes branded on your meat or fish by a stovetop or electric griddle? Partly it's the instant visual memory of that first delicious charbroiled steak that makes our mouths water. Partly, as we all know, the sizzle sells the steak. But most of all, what makes grilled food undeniably toothsome is the caramelization produced by the intense heat of the raised ridges, which in turn push a little river of juice into the valley below. The succulence of quickly seared grilled food rivals that of food prepared by charbroiling. Indoor grilling lacks only the alluring flavor of wood smoke and the flexibility of cooking low and slow. Therein lies the difference between grilling and barbecuing.

Speed and simplicity aside, the beauty of the indoor grill is that it knows no season. This is also true of the produce market. We now import most tropical fruits and spring vegetables year-round, and with our own warmer winters, some local growing seasons are lengthening. The considerable and admirable American interest in lighter, healthier meals does more than make grilling indoors more appealing. Dishes like Carol's Tropical Turkey Salad (page 202) and Ham Steak with Peach Chutney (page 68) in midwinter are not only possible but a welcome change from the steaming stew pot.

The all-year indoor use of an electric grill or rotisserie also allows us to hang on to vestiges of the fun of gathering family and friends around the "fire." Cooking away from the kitchen stove in the family room, dining room, or balcony means we can still watch, smell, and hear the sizzle together—and isn't that the best of it?

Most of the recipes in this book can be prepared both indoors and outdoors, grilled or barbecued, with or without the flavor of smoke, rain or shine. They are all quick to cook, and except for readying the grill, most can be ready in jig time, like Grouper Ti-Malice (page 122) and Chicken Breasts with Peppered Chèvre and Olives (page 90). There are many suggestions for accompaniments in the recipe introductions and the vegetable chapter (page 189), and most can be prepared alongside the main course, making meals even simpler and cleaning up a snap.

There are dishes for the traditionalist, like Barbecued Baby Back Ribs (page 64) and Whole Trout Stuffed with Herbs and Toasted Hazelnuts (page 142), and dishes for the more adventurous, such as Moroccan Cornish Hen (page 94) and Peppered Buffalo Steak (page 70). Since both grilling and barbecuing are practiced worldwide, there are many ethnic recipes, including East Indian Lamb Patties (page 52) and Tokyo Tuna with Soba Noodles (page 138), which confirm that Americans are not alone in their appreciation of the good life. We hope you will enjoy these quick and healthy dishes with a Big Taste!

Barbara Witt

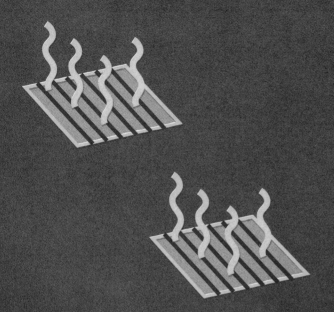

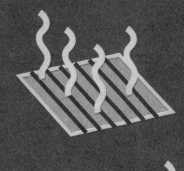

george foreman's big book of grilling, barbecue, and rotisserie

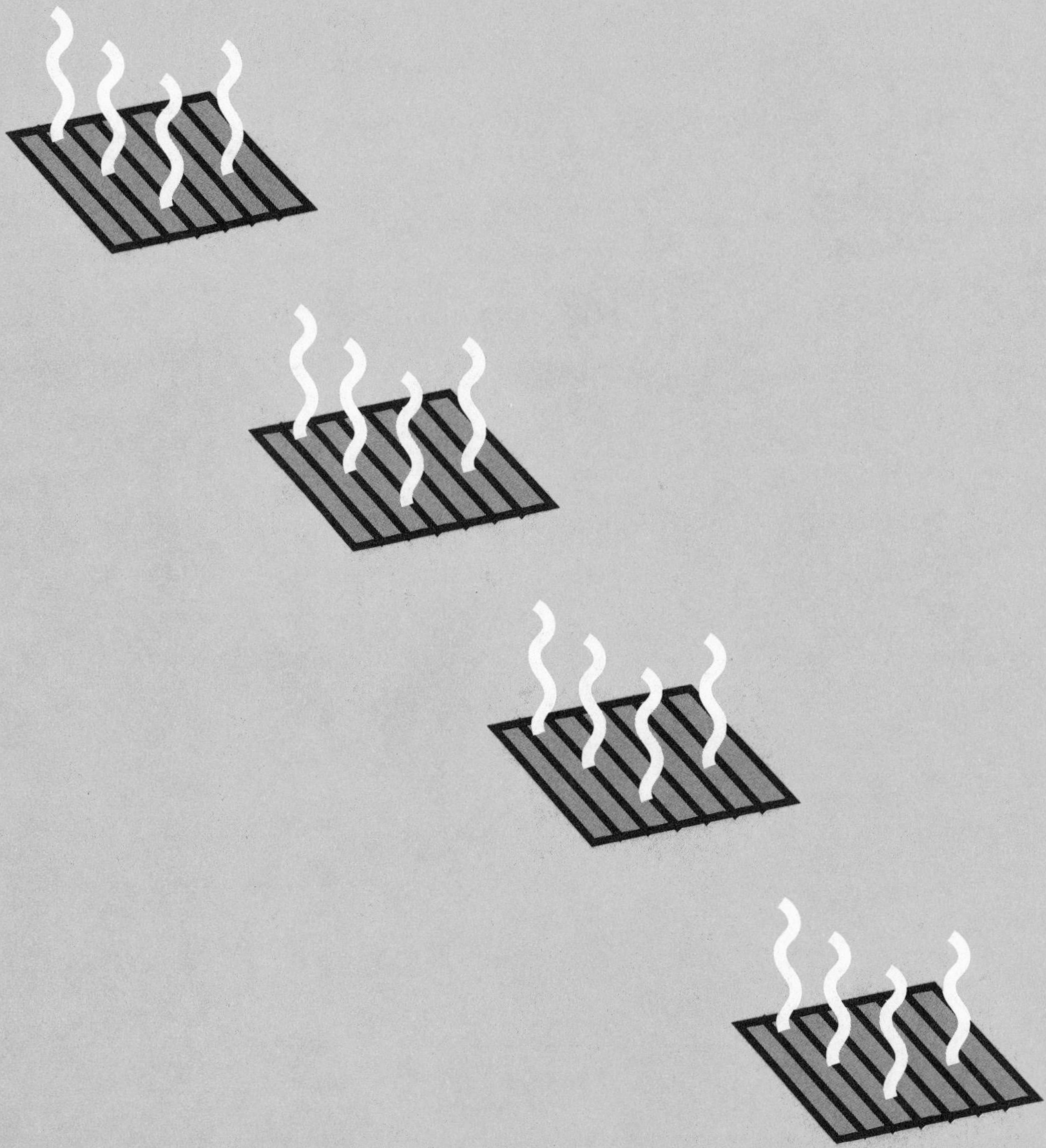

About Equipment

I f you've ever doubted the extent of enthusiasm for grilling in America, you need only check out the Web sites devoted to nothing else or turn the pages of a mail-order equipment catalog. There's a gadget designed to quell every irritant, muzzle every expletive: from a clever flexible grid basket to trap odd-shaped food to a krypton flip-up headlamp to keep the nocturnal chef from stubbing his toe. First prize for frivolity goes to a meat thermometer that beeps you as you lounge indoors, watching a game on TV, to let you know your steak is ready. Is that the perfect gift for kill-joys, or what?

But before you start collecting fun gadgets, you should know the basics about the equipment you're cooking on.

Open-Flame Grills •

Whether charcoal or gas, these grills give the best results for the widest range of meat, poultry, or fish, whether they require fast or slow cooking methods. Basically, you can cook burgers, steaks, and hot dogs outdoors over the simplest of rigs, but if you're serious about success with a wide range of food, look for the following features in your equipment: a charcoal unit large enough to allow for at least two zones of heat; a gas unit with dual flame control; a cover to keep flare-ups to a minimum; a grate that can be adjusted to varying heights above the flame; a fire door to allow adding more coals; and, preferably, a side shelf or rack to keep tools handy. Don't forget to buy a cover to keep the rust away.

Indoor and Outdoor E-Grills •

The outdoor electric grill has a higher wattage than the countertop indoor model and has a well-insulated cover to reflect the heat evenly. It is intended for use where open flames are prohibited—on apartment balconies or patios, for instance, or on a townhouse deck. It does a very credible job of cooking food that you would normally prepare under a broiler because it is hotter than your household range; however, it is not intended for the kind of long, slow, indirect cooking you can achieve on an adjustable open flame. Happily, steaks, chops, chicken, and fish do just as well on these grills as on an outdoor gas grill. Look for accurate temperature control, sturdiness, and good looks. This is in-your-face equipment. Outsize casters for moving it to and from tableside and a convenient cover hook are both desirable features. A flat griddle plate to cover the ridged grid will allow you to cook a dandy pancake or ham and egg breakfast on your balcony. If your interior wiring can handle such high-heat equipment (close to 1,800 watts), a portable e-grill can make an indoor dinner party, since cooking tableside is a lot of fun. Despite their high heat, these units don't smoke noticeably, if at all.

The kitchen counter electric grill is a smaller version of the unit described above. It also cooks from the element just below the grid and is therefore best for quickly prepared foods you might otherwise prepare in a skillet over high heat or under the broiler. The wattage, though lower than for the outdoor model, is high enough to sear a nice, crusty exterior while sealing in moisture. If the grill has a lid that can be lowered, the food will cook in half the time, but meat must be boneless for even cooking. These units are attractive, and their nonstick surfaces are very easy to clean. They have the added advantage of draining off excess fat, but with today's lean meat you have to be careful you don't end up with a paper-dry exterior. A thin coating of oil is generally called for to prevent that.

Rotisseries •

Thank heaven, they are back, as nothing does a better job than an electric rotisserie on small roasts and birds. They are not effective for tough cuts of meat, however, because the heating elements are too close to the surface of the food, which will char before it cooks throughout. But with beef, lamb, or pork loin roasts, they do a superb job, producing a delicious crust and keeping the interior moist. Chicken, duck, and small turkeys cook perfectly. Most units have a kabob accessory and a basket for grilling vegetables. Look for a unit compact enough to keep out on your counter for frequent use, and check it out for the simplicity of inserting and removing the spit mechanism. A hot 10-pound turkey will take up the width of the spit and can be difficult to grab hold of. Temperature control can be a problem and so far has not been solved. Some units allow you to turn off one or more of the heating elements, which is a move in the right direction. What we'd like to see is thermostatic control of the elements themselves, which is a refinement we suspect will come in future deluxe models. Right now we're just happy to have rotisseries back.

Accessories •

For the charcoal grill, we're fond of the chimney-style starter requiring only one sheet of newspaper and a match. The smell, taste, and residual chemicals from liquid flame starters are nasty and a safety hazard. We also recommend a covered waterproof container for storing charcoal (which somehow manages to be left out only on rainy nights). A small garbage can with a clamp-on lid is perfect and raccoon proof.

For either style of outdoor grill, invest in a clip-on light so you can see your way past twilight. Tongs are essential. Kitchen supply shops are now carrying cheap restaurant kitchen tongs in varying lengths. They work better than fancy, expensive ones and are easily replaced. If you don't want to invest in a basket for turning burgers, fish, or small food that might drop through the grate, pick up a piece of fine-mesh screening at the hardware store, cut it to fit the grate, and keep it oiled. At least one heavy asbestos-lined oven mitt will protect you from brutal burns—two are better. You will not regret having a couple of sturdy, heatproof, washable trays for carrying things to and from the kitchen, and finally, but most important, an instant-read meat thermometer is a must.

Checking on Doneness

Throughout this book we've given guidelines for the amount of time it takes to cook food on any type of grill. We make no apology for any inaccuracies because the variables are enormous. Different equipment, different heat intensity, different thickness of food, different preferences and opinions all make it impossible to hit a bull's-eye. Here's the best advice we can give.

- Buy a good instant-read meat thermometer.

- Use this age-old, but professional, thumb test for smaller cuts of meat, poultry, and fish. Hold up your left hand with your thumb relaxed. Press the pad under your thumb with your right thumb. That's the way meat feels when it's still raw. Move your left thumb across your palm all the way to the right. That's the way meat feels when it's overcooked or, you might say, well-done. Halfway in between is medium-rare. This test works amazingly well for all but roasts. Practice.

- Use this chart with your meat thermometer for the most accurate results. Keep in mind that the temperature will rise 5 to 10 degrees after the meat is removed from the heat.

Temperature	Doneness	Meat
120°	Rare	Beef, Lamb, Tuna
130°	Medium-Rare	Beef, Lamb
135°	Medium	Beef, Lamb, Most Fish, Veal
150°	Medium-Well	Beef, Lamb, Pork, and Poultry Breasts
165°	Well-Done	Poultry Dark Meat

The Pantry

Many of the recipes in this book have international overtones requiring ethnic ingredients. Thanks to the increasing diversity of America, most are available in regular supermarkets or specialty food stores. However, if you're lucky enough to live where there are still independent ethnic markets, no doubt you enjoy shopping in them. Here are some things to look for.

Asian

Soba (buckwheat) noodles
Sake—Japanese rice liquor
Japanese ponzu sauce
Japanese yakitori sauce
Japanese wasabi powder
Rice wine vinegar
Toasted sesame oil
Plain sesame oil
Thai or Vietnamese fish sauce
    (*nam pla* or *nuoc mam*)
Hot chili sauce (Thai Sriracha is great)
Hot dried red chilies
Chinese hoisin sauce
Chinese plum sauce
Chinese five-spice powder
Unsweetened coconut milk

Latin

Pico de Gallo, powdered (mixed chilies)
Chipotles en adobo
    (chipotle peppers in sauce)
Mexican hot sauces—red and green

Middle Eastern

Pomegranate syrup

Italian

Penne rigate—pasta
Polenta (instant is OK)
Anchovies—flat
Roasted red peppers
Olivada—black olive paste

General

Capers
Sherry vinegar
Raspberry vinegar
Balsamic vinegar
Peanut oil—cold-pressed
Liquid smoke
Poivre Irise—mixed peppercorns
Ginger preserves—British
Hot sauces—Caribbean, fruit based

Mail-Order Sources

Specialty Meats •

Summerfield Farm, 10044 James Monroe Highway, Culpepper, VA 22701,
   1-800-898-3276

Allen Brothers, Inc., 3737 S. Halsted Street, Chicago, IL 60609,
   1-800-957-0111, www.allenbrothers.com

D'Artagnan, St. Paul Avenue, Jersey City, NJ 07306, 1-800-DARTAGN

Aidell's Sausage Company, 1625 Alvarado Street, San Leandro, CA 94577,
   1-800-546-5795

Specialty Vegetables •

Diamond Organics, P.O. Box 2159, Freedom, CA 95019, 1-888-ORGANIC,
   www.diamondorganics.com

Indian Rock Produce, 530 California Road, Quakerstown, PA 18951,
   1-888-302-6182

Herbs and Spices •

Penzey's Ltd., P.O. Box 933, Muskego, WI 53150, 1-800-741-7787,
   www.penzeys.com

Texas Spice Company, P.O. Box 3769, Austin, TX 78764, 1-800-880-8007

Colorado Spice Company, 5030 Nome Street, Denver, CO 80239, 1-800-67SPICE

Frieda's, Inc., P.O. Box 58488, Los Angeles, CA 90058, 1-800-241-1771

Sauces

Mo Hotta Mo Betta, P.O. Box 4136, San Luis Obispo, CA 93403, 1-800-462-3220

American Spoon Foods, 1668 Clarion Ave., Petoskey, MI 49770, 1-800-222-5886

Asian Ingredients

Oriental Pantry, 423 Great Road, Acton, MA 01720, 1-800-828-0368,
www.orientalpantry.com

Web Sites to Check Out

www.deandeluca.com   www.worldspice.com

www.sfherb.com   www.chefscatalog.com

www.ethnicgrocer.com   www.grilllovers.com

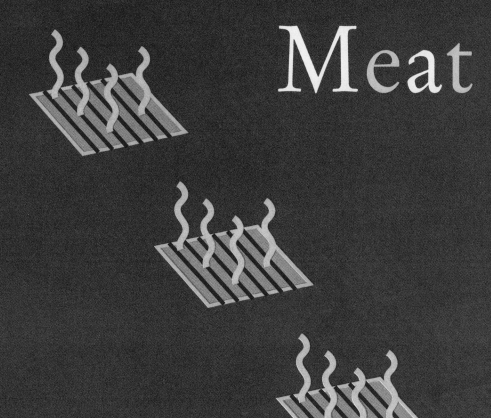

Meat

Kingwood Skirt Steak with Grilled Bananas

Strip Steak in the Style of Kobe

Fiery Orange Sesame Flank Steak

Skewered Beef Tenderloin Oregano

Rib Roast with Rosemary and Roasted Garlic Wine Sauce

Veal Chops in Cider with Grilled Apples

Veal Chops Olivada with Rosemary Potatoes and Gremolata

Lamb Chops Chinois with Pineapple

Lamb Kabobs with Roasted Beets and Figs

East Indian Lamb Patties

Leg of Lamb with Rosemary and Anchovies

Rum Craisin Venison Chops

Butterflied Pork Chops with Apricots

Pork Tenderloin with Cranberry Glaze

Barbecued Baby Back Ribs

Italian Sausage on Polenta Verdure

Ham Steak with Peach Chutney

Peppered Buffalo Steak

Rabbit with Vidalia Onion Mustard Sauce

Kingwood Skirt Steak with Grilled Bananas

There's a touch of Texas and a touch of the Caribbean in this recipe—and what a happy combination. Restaurant chefs have rediscovered skirt steak, but it's a bit hard to find in supermarkets. Keep pestering your butcher because it's a truly delicious cut, similar to flank steak but with more marbling and a beefier flavor. If you can't find skirt steak, you may substitute any cut of beef suitable for grilling.

Various dried chilies in cellophane bags can now be found in quality supermarkets, although usually hidden from plain view. If you're fortunate enough to have a Latin market nearby, you'll have no trouble finding a variety of chilies, and you may even unearth a bag of dried *hoja santa*—fresh would be a real coup, as would be the distinctive and mysterious flavor it adds.

Serves 4

Dry Rub:

1 tablespoon commercial chili powder (see Cook's Notes)

2 teaspoons ancho chili powder

1 teaspoon hot chili powder or cayenne

1 teaspoon dried oregano

1 *hoja santa* leaf, crushed, optional

½ teaspoon ground cinnamon

¼ teaspoon ground cloves

2 teaspoons coarse salt

3 garlic cloves

2 tablespoons canola oil

1½ pounds skirt steak, trimmed

1 tablespoon unsalted butter, melted

31

2 medium ripe bananas, peeled and split lengthwise
freshly grated nutmeg
3 fresh poblano, pasilla, or New Mexico peppers
salt to taste
lime wedges for garnish

In a food processor or spice mill, grind the dry rub ingredients together. Set aside in a small dish.

Add the garlic to the oil with a garlic press. Set aside.

Rub the dry rub into the steak thoroughly on both sides. Wrap loosely in aluminum foil and leave for an hour at room temperature or longer in the refrigerator.

Drizzle the melted butter over the bananas and dust them very lightly with nutmeg. Be sparing—nutmeg is very intense.

Stem and seed the peppers and cut them lengthwise where the ribs are marked. Lightly oil them with your fingers. Grill them on a stovetop, electric, or outdoor grill, skin side down. If your grill has a lid, lower it. Cook the peppers until they're charred but not soft, and toss them in a plastic bag.

Rub the steak with the garlic oil and place on the grill with the bananas. Cook about 4 minutes on each side for a rare to medium-rare steak. The bananas should pick up their stripes sooner. Be careful not to cook them to the soft stage or they'll fall apart. Move them off the heat as soon as they're hot and tender. While waiting for the steak to cook, lift the skins off the peppers and season them lightly with salt.

Slice the steak thinly on the diagonal, against the grain. Overlap the slices down the center of a serving platter. Surround the meat with alternating bananas and peppers. Distribute the lime wedges around the edge.

cook's notes: To turn whole dried peppers into powder, simply stem and seed them and pulverize them in a food processor or spice mill.

Commercial chili powder is a mixture of dried chilies and other spices, one being cumin. If you are using pure chili powder, add ½ teaspoon dried cumin to the herb rub.

● **nutritional breakdown (per serving)**

Calories: 476	Carbohydrates: 23 g	Protein: 43 g	Fat: 24 g
Saturated fat: 8 g	% calories from fat: 46%	Cholesterol: 79 mg	Sodium: 722 mg

Strip Steak in the Style of Kobe

A good lesson to be learned from the culinary habits of the Pacific Rim is that steak doesn't have to be Texas size to be enjoyed. Serving the meat sliced and artistically fanned out on a plate in the Japanese manner grants high-quality meat the stardom it deserves and brings quantity into sensible perspective. The seasoned soy dip adds sparkle to the natural flavor of beef, and the pretty green wad of wasabi lights a very pleasant fire on the tongue when dipped into judiciously.

Serve a bowl of steamed rice topped with slivered scallions to gather up the juices, and grill asparagus spears and shiitake mushrooms to make this a perfectly satisfying and healthful meal.

Serves 4

Dipping Sauce:
- 5 tablespoons Japanese soy sauce
- 5 tablespoons sake
- 1 teaspoon Asian sesame oil
- 4 garlic cloves, smashed and minced
- 2 teaspoons light brown sugar

- 1 tablespoon wasabi powder
- 1 pound strip steak, 1¼ inches thick

Combine the dipping sauce ingredients in a small microwave-safe dish and heat on high for 1 minute to melt the sugar. Stir and set aside in 4 little individual dishes to cool.

Drizzle just enough water over the wasabi powder to make a thick paste and roll it between your fingers into 4 little balls, then place them on a dish. Cover the dish with plastic wrap and set aside for about 15 minutes to develop the flavor.

Cook the steak on a stovetop or electric grill about 3 minutes per side or for 5 minutes total on a hinged grill with the lid down. On an outdoor grill over white-ash coals, the steak should test medium-rare within 10 minutes.

Slice the steak thinly into 4 servings and neatly overlap the slices on the plates. Place one of the marbles of wasabi on each plate and set a bowl of dipping sauce alongside.

● **nutritional breakdown (per serving)**

| Calories: 242 | Carbohydrates: 7 g | Protein 27 g | Fat 9 g |
| Saturated fat: 3 g | % calories from fat: 32% | Cholesterol: 53 mg | Sodium: 1,210 mg |

Fiery Orange Sesame Flank Steak

Flank steak is an ideal choice for grilling and marries very well with zesty marinades or barbecue sauce. This one has Korean overtones with a citrus twist and can be fiery or not, depending on how much chili sauce you add. Remember that the heat won't permeate the meat all the way through, and although the crispy crust is a big part of flank steak's appeal, the marinade flavors will be blurred a little by the necessary intensity of the grill's heat. Be generous with the seasonings. Taste the mixture and adjust the proportions to your personal preference. If you love it, double the recipe and refrigerate it for using on your next chicken or pork dinner. You might even consider grilling two steaks at once and storing one to slice and serve cold. Rare flank steak makes a super sandwich and is equally wonderful over noodles or slivered on top of a spinach salad.

Serves 4

Marinade:

4 garlic cloves, smashed and minced

6 scallions, white parts minced with 1 inch of the green

3 tablespoons light brown sugar

1 tablespoon sesame seeds, toasted

grated zest of 1 orange

⅓ cup soy sauce

¼ cup dry sherry

1 tablespoon frozen orange juice concentrate

1 tablespoon Asian sesame oil

1½ teaspoons hot Asian chili sauce, or to taste

1 flank steak, about 1¼ pounds

coarse salt and freshly ground black pepper to taste

Combine all the marinade ingredients in a glass 2-cup measure and heat it in the microwave to dissolve the sugar and soften the garlic. Taste for seasoning. If it isn't spicy enough, add more chili sauce. If it isn't sweet enough, add more sugar. If too sweet, add a dash of rice vinegar. Allow the mixture to cool.

Drop the flank steak into a large freezer bag and pour in the cooled marinade. Seal the bag and refrigerate for at least 2 hours, preferably overnight. Pour the marinade into a small saucepan or glass measuring cup and bring it to a boil on the stove or in the microwave. Reserve it for dipping the meat at the table.

Season the meat with the salt and black pepper. Sear it on a stovetop, electric, or outdoor grill for 3 to 4 minutes on each side, which should produce a perfect rare to medium-rare steak. If you overcook this cut of meat, it will be abysmally dry.

Slice the steak very thinly on the diagonal and always against the grain. Pass the reheated marinade for dipping.

● **nutritional breakdown (per serving)**

Calories: 386	Carbohydrates: 18 g	Protein: 38g	Fat: 17g
Saturated fat: 6 g	% calories from fat: 39%	Cholesterol: 63 mg	Sodium: 1,551 mg

Skewered Beef Tenderloin Oregano

The beef we buy today just isn't the same as when Mother was a girl. It's no longer dry aged or well marbled and therefore has lost the rich, juicy, uniquely beefy flavor that made Americans lust for steak for decades. For that reason, the elegant tenderloin has regained popularity—without the béarnaise sauce. When cooked rare, it can always be counted on to be buttery tender, and it doesn't seem so pricey after all when you realize there's neither fat nor bone waste. It's a cut well suited to marinades that enhance its less robust flavor, so it's a splendid quick-cook choice for the grill. This spicy Mediterranean marinade lends real character to the meat and, if cooked with care, helps to retain its moisture. Serve these attractive kabobs on slabs of good bakery bread brushed with olive oil and garlic and toasted crisp on the grill.

Serves 4

Marinade:

3 tablespoons extra-virgin olive oil

4 garlic cloves, smashed and minced

3 tablespoons minced onion

½ teaspoon salt

½ teaspoon freshly ground black pepper

¼ teaspoon dried red pepper flakes

⅓ cup dry red wine

¼ cup balsamic vinegar

1½ tablespoons fresh oregano leaves

1½ pounds beef tenderloin, cut into 24 1¼-inch cubes

16 shallots or tiny onions, peeled

16 large cherry tomatoes

Heat the oil in a small saucepan and sauté the garlic, onion, salt, pepper, and red pepper flakes until the onion and garlic are soft. Add the wine, vinegar, and oregano and simmer gently for 3 minutes. Set aside to cool.

Put the tenderloin cubes in a large plastic freezer bag. When the marinade is cool, pour it over the meat. Seal the bag and refrigerate 3 to 4 hours or overnight.

Blanch the shallots in the microwave with a small amount of water, covered, for a minute or two, or until they are only partially cooked.

Using either water-soaked wooden skewers or the metal ones supplied with a rotisserie, start threading the skewers, beginning and ending with the meat. If you are grilling outdoors or on an indoor electric or stovetop grill, thread 2 skewers per person, each with 3 cubes of meat alternated with the tomatoes and shallots. If you are using a rotisserie, you can probably thread all 6 cubes of meat on one skewer, but you'll be short 1 tomato and 1 shallot per person. Just put 2 meat cubes together in the center or use all 8 skewers, pushing the contents tightly to the middle.

These kabobs will take only about 5 minutes over white-ash coals or on an indoor grill with a lid. On the rotisserie, they will take about 15 minutes.

● **nutritional breakdown (per serving)**

Calories: 356	Carbohydrates: 13 g	Protein: 38 g	Fat: 16g
Saturated fat: 5 g	% calories from fat: 41%	Cholesterol: 107 mg	Sodium: 186 mg

Rib Roast with Rosemary and Roasted Garlic Wine Sauce

If your kitchen can accommodate another piece of equipment, it's worth buying a rotisserie just for small roasts and plump birds. The high heat of the elements and their close proximity to the surface of the meat renders a crusty exterior and a rare to medium center in less time than the oven. A rib roast of beef is not for weekday suppers, and when you choose to serve it to honored guests, you'll probably welcome having your oven free for other things. If you have a spit on your charcoal grill, you can produce a memorable feast, but you'll have to forgo the flavorful dark drippings that punch up this sauce. An electric rotisserie is the next best thing to the Tuscan fireplace spit that turns the meat slowly in front of the flame, allowing the precious juices to drip into a pan below. Well, we Americans can't have everything now, can we?

Serves 6 to 8

1 boned and tied 3-rib roast, from the small end, about 6 pounds

Seasoning Paste:
4 garlic cloves, smashed and minced
1½ teaspoons dried rosemary
1 teaspoon coarse salt
1 teaspoon coarsely ground black pepper
1 tablespoon extra-virgin olive oil

Sauce:

1 large head garlic or 2 small, roasted (see box on page 127)

olive oil

1¼ cups full-bodied red wine

⅔ cup canned or homemade beef broth

salt and freshly ground black pepper to taste

Rinse the meat and pat it dry. Combine all the ingredients for the seasoning paste in a mortar and crush it thoroughly with the pestle. Coat the exposed meat completely and use the rest of the paste to season the exterior fat. Make certain the meat is well tied and fasten it to the spit rods according to the manufacturer's instructions. If your rotisserie has a thermostat, set it on high and sear the meat well. Reduce the heat, or the number of active elements, and continue cooking until an instant-read thermometer registers 115°. Allow the roast to rest with the motor off and the door closed for 15 to 20 minutes. By this time, the internal temperature will have risen 5 to 10 degrees and the meat will be rare and juicy. A roast of this size will not take much longer than an hour to cook to perfection.

While the roast is resting, make the sauce. Squeeze out all the garlic from the roasted head and dribble in a touch of olive oil to make a thick, smooth paste. Pull the drip tray out from under the meat, replacing it with a piece of aluminum foil, and pour off all but a couple of tablespoons of the fat. Reserve and refrigerate this fat for making hash from the leftovers or for roasting potatoes. Put the drip tray over a low burner and pour in the wine. Allow it to come to a simmer. Scrape up all the brown specks on the bottom of the pan and reduce the wine by half. Pour the contents of the drip tray into a small saucepan, scraping the bottom thoroughly. Add the beef broth and reduce again until the sauce looks slightly syrupy and there are about 1¼ cups remaining. Season the sauce with pepper, but taste before using salt. Canned beef broth can be overly salty.

Slice the meat thinly and pass the hot sauce separately.

nutritional breakdown (per serving for 6)

Calories: 840	Carbohydrates: 4 g	Protein: 52 g	Fat: 68 g
Saturated fat: 27 g	% calories from fat: 24%	Cholesterol: 191 mg	Sodium: 362 mg

(per serving for 8)

Calories: 567	Carbohydrates: 2 g	Protein: 35 g	Fat: 45 g
Saturated fat: 18 g	% calories from fat: 71%	Cholesterol: 127 mg	Sodium: 241 mg

About Seasoning and Flavor

Dry Spice Rubs

An outside rub of salt and pepper is a given and need only be done just before cooking. Beyond that, the herb and spice options are endless and open to personal taste and experimentation. For optimum flavor, check your spice rack and replace those weakened by time. Apply dry rubs a couple of hours before cooking. Start by simply mixing salt and pepper with your favorite herb—rosemary, thyme, oregano, sage, basil—and add a little garlic powder and paprika for depth and color. If you're fond of the southwestern taste, use chili powder, cumin, oregano, cayenne, and garlic powder.

Note: Most dry rubs tend to burn on contact with the high heat of electric grills, so we've hesitated using them in this book.

Seasoning Pastes

We find paste rubs more satisfactory than dry rubs, especially on today's lean meats. They also work better on electric grills. Adding a little oil to a dry rub constitutes a basic seasoning paste, but you can also mix in "wet" flavor enhancements, such as minced garlic and ginger, mustard, anchovy, olive, tamarind, or sun-dried tomato paste. These flavors won't penetrate the meat much beneath the surface, but they will add zest to the seared crust or skin. The trick here is to keep it simple. Elaborate concoctions won't receive the notice you might think they deserve.

Veal Chops in Cider with Grilled Apples

When shorts give your legs goose bumps and the apples are tumbling from the trees, pull on your jeans and sweatshirt and grill this delicious autumn dinner. Surely by then you're pretty weary of barbecued chicken and potato salad. A taste of wintry comfort food should be just the ticket, and for once, the heat of the grill will actually feel good. The succulence of this seasonal recipe won't be lost if you have to grill the chops indoors. We can't think of a better accompaniment than garlic mashed potatoes.

Serves 4

4 veal loin chops, 1¼ inches thick

2½ cups sweet apple cider

¼ cup cider vinegar

¼ cup brandy, optional

1 tablespoon + 2 teaspoons sugar

1 tablespoon fresh lemon juice

¾ teaspoon dried thyme

¼ teaspoon coarse salt

dash of Tabasco

2 Golden Delicious apples, peeled, cored, and thickly sliced

2 medium red onions, peeled and thickly sliced

salt and freshly ground black pepper to taste

¼ cup heavy cream (see Cook's Note)

Make several tiny slits in the veal chops with the tip of a sharp paring knife. Place them in a freezer bag and pour in 1 cup of the cider and all the vinegar. Seal the bag and allow the chops to marinate 2 to 3 hours or overnight.

In a glass 2-cup measure, reduce the remaining cider, brandy, sugar, lemon juice, thyme, coarse salt, and Tabasco in the microwave on high until about 1¼ cups remain. Set aside.

Sprinkle the veal chops and the apple and onion slices with salt and pepper, and cook on a stovetop or electric grill for about 15 minutes, or until the chops are still springy and the apple and onion slices are soft and charred. This should take about 10 minutes on a banked white-ash charcoal fire if the meat is seared first for a couple of minutes on each side. In all methods, brush the meat with the reduced sauce several times during the last 5 minutes of cooking time.

Reheat the remaining sauce. Add the cream and simmer only until it slightly thickens. Serve the chops with the apples and onions to one side and pour the sauce over the veal.

cook's note: You can use evaporated skim milk instead of cream, or you can enrich the sauce with 2 or 3 tablespoons of cold butter. Cut it in pieces and whisk it in rapidly.

nutritional breakdown (per serving)

Calories: 449	Carbohydrates: 31 g	Protein: 33 g	Fat: 43 g
Saturated fat: 10 g	% calories from fat: 43%	Cholesterol: 152 mg	Sodium: 353 mg

Veal Chops Olivada with Rosemary Potatoes and Gremolata

What could be better today than both easy and delicious? This one-dish dinner will take less time to prepare than starting up the grill, and all you need are a few basic ingredients. Garnish the veal with the classic Italian gremolata and serve with a pristine *insalata mista* and a chilled bottle of Pinot Grigio. *Ecco!*

Serves 4

3 large baking potatoes, or 4 Yukon Golds, peeled (see Cook's Note)
½ cup canned low-sodium chicken broth
½ teaspoon dried rosemary
salt and freshly ground black pepper to taste
4 thick veal loin chops
small jar olivada (black olive paste)
3 garlic cloves, pressed
3 tablespoons extra-virgin olive oil

Gremolata:
grated zest of 1 lemon
3 tablespoons minced parsley
2 garlic cloves, minced

Thinly trim off the rounded side of each potato and cut them in thick lengthwise slices. Place them in a large, shallow, microwave-safe dish. Add the chicken broth, rosemary, and salt and pepper. Cook on high for 3 to 4 minutes, or until the potatoes are half cooked. Drain and set aside.

Make a wide pocket in each chop with the tip of a sharp utility knife. Spread each pocket generously with the olivada. Combine the pressed garlic with the olive oil and lightly rub the chops with this mixture. Season with salt and pepper and set aside for the grill.

Combine the ingredients for the gremolata in a small dish and reserve.

Spray or rub the potatoes lightly with olive oil and sprinkle with a little more rosemary if you like. Season with salt and pepper. Grill the potato slices first (unless you have a large outdoor grill) until they are crusty brown and soft in the center. Keep them warm in a low oven or to one side of the coals.

Cook the veal chops on a stovetop, electric, or outdoor grill for 5 to 6 minutes per side, or just until the meat springs back slightly. Serve immediately with the warm potatoes and dust the chops with the gremolata.

cook's note: Both grilled zucchini halves and artichoke hearts go splendidly with this dish—either with or instead of the potatoes.

● **nutritional breakdown (per serving)**

Calories: 509	Carbohydrates: 28 g	Protein: 34 g	Fat: 28 g
Saturated fat: 8 g	% calories from fat: 50%	Cholesterol: 131 mg	Sodium: 631 mg

Lamb Chops Chinois with Pineapple

Lamb chops are drawn to the grill like the proverbial moths to the flame. This Chinese-style basting sauce paints on a lovely glaze and produces a complex sweet and spicy crust. Serve these chops with thick slices of grilled eggplant, charred onions, and rice liberally seasoned with minced cilantro.

Serves 4

Basting Sauce:
- 3 tablespoons Chinese plum sauce
- 2 tablespoons soy sauce
- 2 tablespoons hoisin sauce
- 2 tablespoons dry sherry
- 2 tablespoons canned low-sodium chicken broth
- 1 tablespoon rice vinegar
- 1 tablespoon honey
- 1 teaspoon Asian sesame oil
- ½ teaspoon Chinese five-spice powder
- ½ teaspoon ground ginger
- 2 small hot dried chili peppers, seeded and crushed, or Tabasco to taste
- 3 garlic cloves, smashed and minced

4 to 8 lamb loin chops, 1¼ inches thick
salt and freshly ground black pepper to taste
1 fresh pineapple, peeled, cored, and sealed in a plastic bag (available in the produce section)

Put the basting sauce ingredients in a glass 2-cup measure and microwave on high for 3 minutes. Set aside.

Trim the chops of excess fat. Season with salt and pepper. Cut the pineapple into thick slices, reserving the juice.

Sear the surface of the chops quickly on a hot stovetop, electric, or outdoor grill. Reduce the heat where possible and cook the chops for about 4 minutes more per side for medium-rare. Brush the meat liberally and often with the basting sauce during the final 3 minutes of cooking time. At this point, lay the pineapple slices on the grill. Add some of the juice to the basting sauce and lace the fruit with it as you turn the slices over. This should produce caramelized brown stripes. Serve immediately.

cook's note: This basting sauce works equally well on a rack or leg of lamb.

nutritional breakdown (per serving)

Calories: 456	Carbohydrates: 22 g	Protein: 30 g	Fat: 27 g
Saturated fat: 11 g	% calories from fat: 54%	Cholesterol: 114 mg	Sodium: 402 mg

Lamb Kabobs with Roasted Beets and Figs

There are Middle Eastern overtones to this dish, and why not? The Turks have been grilling lamb over an open fire since the Ottoman Empire. Instead of threading the traditional onion, tomato, and green pepper with the meat, we used figs and roasted beets. This is a real treat when fresh figs are in season, but dried Turkish figs, plumped up in citrus juice, work surprisingly well. Be sure to roast extra beets, douse them well with balsamic vinegar, and store them in the refrigerator for another meal. Serve couscous studded with toasted walnuts and a basket of pita bread with the kabobs.

Serves 4

1 large yellow onion, chopped
⅓ cup extra-virgin olive oil
1 teaspoon ground cinnamon
salt and freshly ground black pepper to taste
1½ pounds lamb loin, cut into 1¼-inch cubes
3 beets, tops trimmed close, roots intact
balsamic vinegar
8 Turkish dried figs or fresh figs in season
orange juice
2 lime slices
mint sprigs for garnish

In a food processor or blender, reduce the onion to a thick, watery pulp. Remove it to a piece of double cheesecloth or strong paper towels, and squeeze out all the juice into a bowl large enough to hold the meat. Add the oil, cinnamon, salt and pepper, and lamb to the onion juice. Cover and marinate the lamb as long as possible, preferably overnight.

Preheat the oven to 375°. Put the beets on the middle oven rack and roast them for about 1½ hours, or until they shrink and the skins shrivel. Allow them to cool enough to be handled and snip off the root. The skins will slip off easily by hand. Slice the beets thickly, sprinkle with salt and pepper, and drizzle generously with balsamic vinegar. Refrigerate.

If you are using dried figs, cover them with orange juice and add 2 slices of lime. Cover and microwave on high for 30 seconds. Allow them to stand long enough to become infused with the citrus and soft enough to be skewered. Drain and cut them in half crosswise. Drizzle them with balsamic vinegar. If you are using fresh figs, omit the citrus soak and simply cut them in half and dress with balsamic vinegar.

Thread the skewers, starting and ending with the lamb. Fasten a slice of beet against the cut side of each fig half.

Cook the kabobs on an indoor rotisserie for 15 to 20 minutes, testing the meat for doneness to assure it remains pink and moist. On an outdoor grill, the kabobs should be ready in about 10 minutes. Serve immediately and garnish with mint sprigs.

cook's note: The beets and figs can be prepared up to 3 days in advance.

● nutritional breakdown (per serving)

Calories: 581	Carbohydrates: 33 g	Protein: 34 g	Fat: 35 g
Saturated fat: 13 g	% calories from fat: 54%	Cholesterol: 128 mg	Sodium: 293 mg

East Indian Lamb Patties

Ground lamb is appealingly inexpensive, but what to do with it doesn't spring quickly to mind. Cooks have no such problem in India, where lamb commonly appears in dishes similar to this one. The preparation is very simple, and the spices are pungent and exotic. Serve these luscious grilled patties with minted yogurt, a bowl of hot garlicky chickpeas tossed with minced onion, and sautéed baby spinach. Put some store-bought chapatis on the grill to reheat.

Serves 4

1 pound ground lamb

¼ cup minced scallions

2 large garlic cloves, minced

3 tablespoons chopped pistachios, optional

2 teaspoons dried mint

2 teaspoons tumeric

1 teaspoon ground allspice

salt to taste

pinch of cayenne, or to taste

1 egg, lightly beaten

2 tablespoons plain yogurt

Combine the lamb with all the other ingredients, working the mixture lightly but thoroughly with your fingers the same way you make a meat loaf. Form the lamb into 4 plump patties without compacting the meat.

Cook the patties on a stovetop, electric, or outdoor grill as you would cook a hamburger. They should not be cooked rare. A barely pink center will guarantee their juiciness.

cook's notes: It's nice to pass around a bowl of low-fat yogurt mixed two to one with light sour cream and seasoned with minced fresh mint leaves.

This dish is a perfect candidate for a company meal, in which case you might want to form the lamb into fat sausage shapes and grill them on short wooden skewers in keeping with their ethnicity.

nutritional breakdown (per serving)

Calories: 275	Carbohydrates: 3 g	Protein: 23 g	Fat: 18 g
Saturated fat: 7 g	% calories from fat: 59%	Cholesterol: 136 mg	Sodium: 239 mg

Leg of Lamb with Rosemary and Anchovies

The harmony of lamb with rosemary, garlic, lemon, and anchovies is unequaled. Add the intangible smoky flavor from an outdoor grill or the crusty surface from an electric rotisserie and it reaches the sublime. We find the spring lamb from Australia, rolled up into a little net sack, to be the ideal size for a small family or company dinner. There should be just enough left over to make a few four-star sandwiches on olive bread moistened with garlic mayonnaise.

Serves 4

1 boneless leg of lamb, preferably Australian, about 5 pounds
salt and freshly ground black pepper to taste
3 garlic cloves, slivered
3 garlic cloves, smashed
3-ounce tin flat anchovy fillets, not drained, minced
2 tablespoons chopped fresh rosemary (see Cook's Note)
¼ cup chopped flat-leaf parsley
grated zest of 1 lemon
extra-virgin olive oil

If there's a net sack around the meat, cut it off and lay the lamb out flat on the cutting board, fat side up. Trim off any excess fat, leaving a thin layer. Sprinkle the exposed surface with salt and pepper. Make a few random tiny, slanted slits in the meat and push in the slivered garlic. Turn the lamb over. Sprinkle the exposed surface with salt and pepper.

In a food processor, combine the smashed garlic, anchovies, 1½ tablespoons of the rosemary, 3 tablespoons of the parsley, and all but a pinch of the lemon zest. Pulse into a semi-paste, drizzling in a bit of olive oil to facilitate the mixing. Smear this seasoning all over the inside of the roast. If you're cooking on a rotisserie, tie the meat securely into its original compact shape with kitchen twine. If you're cooking on an outdoor grill, leave it untied and make a few discreet cuts to flatten the meat for even grilling.

In either case, combine the remaining rosemary, parsley, and lemon zest and press the mixture onto the outside of the lamb. Spray or rub lightly with olive oil.

For the ideal medium-rare center, the roast will take 1 hour and 15 minutes on the rotisserie, or until an instant-read thermometer registers 130°. The meat should stand for 15 minutes before slicing.

On an outdoor grill, cook the meat in the same manner as a steak. It should take 6 to 8 minutes per side but can easily be tested with the tip of a knife to assure it stays pink and moist.

cook's note: If you're cooking over an open fire, toss a few sprigs of rosemary on the coals. The herb-flavored smoke will infuse the lamb.

nutritional breakdown (per serving)

| Calories: 369 | Carbohydrates: 1 g | Protein: 37 g | Fat: 23 g |
| Saturated fat: 10 g | % calories from fat: 57% | Cholesterol: 145 mg | Sodium: 331 mg |

Rum Craisin Venison Chops

Venison chops, cranberries, and dark rum sounded like an enticing combination, and naming it was even harder to resist. Cranberries processed and sweetened like raisins—what will those clever folks at Ocean Spray think of next? The venison loin chops we ordered from our supermarket butcher turned out to be a fresh New Zealand rack of eight ribs with ruby-red meat nuggets on each pristine six-inch bone. It was a roast of pure beauty, as awesome as the sticker shock. But what a rare treat! This special-occasion feast for four can be either grilled outdoors whole, like a rack of lamb, or split between the ribs and speed-grilled indoors or out in the same manner as small steaks or medallions of pork or veal. Either way, low-fat venison should be cooked no further than medium-rare. The tart-sweet, peppery sauce is just enough to moisten and enhance the flavor of the mild and luscious meat and can be made as far ahead as you like.

Serves 4

1 rack of venison
salt and freshly ground black pepper to taste

Sauce:

¼ cup Craisins

¼ cup dark rum, preferably Myers Original Dark

1¼ cups canned low-sodium or homemade beef broth

⅓ cup fruity red wine, such as Merlot or Zinfandel

3 large garlic cloves, smashed

1 large shallot, chopped

¾ teaspoon cracked black pepper

½ teaspoon coarse salt

¼ teaspoon beef extract or flavoring, preferably Lehman Brothers

1 tablespoon raspberry vinegar

1 tablespoon currant jelly

1 tablespoon soft unsalted butter

Rinse the rack of venison and pat dry. If you are cooking it on an indoor grill, cut the rack between the bones into chops, leaving the rib bone intact. Season each chop with salt and pepper. If you are cooking outdoors and prefer grilling the rack whole, season it and cover the bones halfway up with aluminum foil to keep them from burning. Do the same if you are cooking chops over an open flame.

Put the Craisins in a small dish and add the rum. Cover the dish with plastic wrap and set aside.

Pour the broth and wine into a small saucepan and add the garlic, shallot, and pepper. Bring the liquid to a fast boil over high heat. Reduce the heat and simmer about 15 minutes, or until the mixture is reduced to about 1 cup. Strain out the shallot and garlic, pressing down lightly with the back of a spoon to extract as much flavorful juice as possible. Return the liquid to the saucepan and add the salt, beef extract, vinegar, and raspberry and currant jelly. Bring the sauce back to a boil and simmer again for another couple of minutes, or until slightly syrupy. When the Craisins are almost soft, add them to the sauce along with the rum and again bring the sauce to a simmer. In another minute or so, you will be back to about 1 cup of sauce and the alcohol will be burned off. Taste for seasoning and set aside. At this point, you can keep the sauce at room temperature for several hours or refrigerate it. Whisk in the butter just before serving.

If cooking over an open flame, sear the meat on both sides for 1 to 2 minutes, or until a nice brown crust starts to form. Reduce the heat or move the roast away from direct flame and cook for another 10 minutes per side, or until a meat thermometer registers 125° to 130°.

If you cook the chops indoors or out as you would a steak, they will take only 2 to 3 minutes per side. Test one with the tip of a sharp knife before removing them from the grill.

Lightly coat each serving with a drizzle of the sauce and serve immediately.

● **nutritional breakdown (per serving)**

Calories: 357	Carbohydrates: 11 g	Protein: 38 g	Fat: 15 g
Saturated fat: 5 g	% calories from fat: 38%	Cholesterol: 145 mg	Sodium: 1,173 mg

Butterflied Pork Chops with Apricots

Pale pink pork loin looks enticing in the meat case, but we're often disappointed at the table because we instinctively tend to cook it too long. It's tough to break old habits. The "new white meat" no longer carries the risk of trichinosis in this country and should be cooked like the equally lean veal—pink within a narrow gray edge. The stuffing in this recipe could also be a topping for a loin chop, but we like the infusion of flavor it gives the pork when cooked inside. Besides, it makes for a more special presentation. If you don't see butterflied boneless loin chops in the meat case, ask the butcher to cut them for you.

Serves 4

4 boneless pork loin chops, butterflied

Marinade:

2 tablespoons extra-virgin olive oil

4 garlic cloves, smashed and minced

¼ teaspoon Pico de Gallo (see Cook's Notes) or cayenne

¼ teaspoon salt

2 teaspoons grated orange zest

2 tablespoons dry sherry

Stuffing:

8 dried apricots

orange juice

1 tablespoon extra-virgin olive oil

¾ cup minced sweet onion

2 teaspoons minced garlic

1 teaspoon ground cumin

salt and freshly ground black pepper to taste

1 tablespoon minced fresh oregano

4 wooden skewers, 6 inches long (see Cook's Notes)

Put the meat in a large plastic bag. Combine the marinade ingredients and pour over the meat. Seal the bag and marinate overnight if possible.

Cover the apricots with orange juice and microwave on high for 1½ minutes. Set aside to soften.

Heat the oil in a small skillet and sauté the onion until pale golden brown, adding the garlic and cumin halfway through. Season with salt and pepper. Stir in the oregano. Remove from the heat. Drain the apricots, then chop and stir them in.

Open up the chops and spoon the stuffing into each one, placing it close to the fold. Close the edges with skewers. Toothpicks are too short to do the job. If you have only longer skewers, simply break them. If you have none, you can risk leaving the edges open—use tongs to hold them closed when you turn the chops over.

Moisten the chops with the marinade. Indoors on a stovetop or electric grill or outdoors over gas or charcoal, sear the chops over high heat for 1 minute on each side. Lower the heat and grill another 4 to 5 minutes per side. If using a lidded electric grill, cook only 4 to 5 minutes altogether.

cook's notes: Most well-stocked supermarkets carry wooden skewers. They just like to hide them so you'll have to ask.

Pico de Gallo is another one of those convenient pantry items for lovers of spicy food. It's a Mexican mixture of ground dried hot chilies used to season mixed fruit or vegetable salsas called Pico de Gallo Jalisco. It comes in a 4-ounce jar with a red shaker top and can be found in many Latin or specialty food stores.

● **nutritional breakdown (per serving)**

Calories: 467	Carbohydrates: 10 g	Protein: 46 g	Fat: 26 g
Saturated fat: 8 g	% calories from fat: 50%	Cholesterol: 128 mg	Sodium: 239 mg

Pork Tenderloin with Cranberry Glaze

Pork tenderloin is such an easy grill partner. It's boneless, fat free, quick cooking, and portion controlled by Mother Nature. The dual-pack tenderloins are perfect for four people. If their appetites are modest, there could be enough left over for a cold pork sandwich—the next day's cook's treat. Once again, be warned that overcooking these lean little darlings can be disastrous. Serve this festive pork with lightly buttered wild rice tossed with grilled shallots and petite peas.

Serves 4

2 pork tenderloins, about 10 ounces each
salt and freshly ground black pepper to taste

Glaze:

1 cup whole cranberry sauce
1 large shallot, chopped
1 red jalapeño pepper, stemmed and partially seeded
1 tablespoon fresh lemon juice
¼ cup fruity red wine
2 teaspoons ginger preserves, British import label
1½ tablespoons minced fresh rosemary, or 1½ teaspoons dried
1 tablespoon canola oil
Tabasco to taste, if needed

rosemary sprigs for garnish

Rinse the tenderloins, pat dry, and season with salt and pepper.

Puree the glaze ingredients in a food processor. Pour into a microwave-safe bowl and reduce on high for 5 minutes. The glaze should be thick and syrupy. If it's too thin, put it back in the microwave in 1-minute increments. Should it become too thick, simply stir in a bit more wine. Taste for seasoning and adjust, if necessary. The glaze should be slightly tart and spicy. Remember that sweetness will predominate when it caramelizes on the grill, so you might want to start out on the tart side. Also, a glaze provides a glossy crust but does not permeate the meat. If you love spicy food, heat this up a bit more with Tabasco.

Cook the tenderloins on a medium-hot indoor or outdoor grill for 8 to 10 minutes, basting heavily with the glaze during the last 5 minutes. An instant-read thermometer should reach 150° for a pink interior.

Heat any remaining glaze. Slice the meat on the diagonal to serve and drizzle the glaze over the top. Garnish with rosemary sprigs.

nutritional breakdown (per serving)

Calories: 385	Carbohydrates: 33 g	Protein: 33 g	Fat: 13 g
Saturated fat: 3 g	% calories from fat: 34%	Cholesterol: 97 mg	Sodium: 247 mg

Barbecued Baby Back Ribs

Spareribs require long cooking and low indirect heat to reach succulent and tender perfection. Most indoor grills are simply too hot, and even if they're thermostatically controlled, the element is too close to the meat, which can easily become dry and stringy. What's needed to do the job properly is a gas or charcoal grill, because the flame can be regulated or the coals well banked. Oven roasting indoors is a good substitute, and the tender little baby backs can be finished off nicely in the large basket of a rotisserie. When you're hungering for a quick rib fix, give them a head start in the microwave and save the glazing for a blast in the rotisserie or under the broiler.

Serves 4

4 pounds pork baby back ribs
salt and freshly ground black pepper to taste
1 cup canned low-sodium chicken broth

Barbecue Sauce:
3 tablespoons canola oil
1 small or ½ large onion, chopped
6 garlic cloves, chopped
1 teaspoon dry mustard
1 teaspoon liquid smoke
⅓ cup reduced-sodium soy sauce
⅓ cup spicy ketchup
2 tablespoons Worcestershire sauce
1 tablespoon hoisin sauce
¼ cup cider vinegar

1 tablespoon hot sauce, or to taste

3 tablespoons honey, or to taste

salt and freshly ground black pepper to taste

Season the ribs with salt and pepper and place them in a microwave-safe rectangular dish in a single layer, bone side up. If they all won't fit in without crowding, precook them in relays. Pour in enough of the chicken broth to cover the bottom of the dish, cover it tightly with plastic wrap, and cook on high for 10 minutes. Drain and set aside.

Heat the oil in a small saucepan and sauté the onion and garlic until soft. Stir in the mustard. Add the rest of the sauce ingredients and simmer the mixture for 10 minutes. Cool. Either process to puree or strain through a fine-mesh sieve, pressing as much of the garlic and onion through as you can.

Put the ribs in the large basket of a rotisserie, under the broiler, or on an outside grill. Once they start to crisp and brown, repeatedly baste them with the sauce. The ribs should be tender and pulling away from the bone in about 15 minutes.

● **nutritional breakdown (per serving)**

Calories: 818	Carbohydrates: 30 g	Protein: 43 g	Fat: 60 g
Saturated fat: 18 g	% calories from fat: 65%	Cholesterol: 116 mg	Sodium: 1,618 mg

Italian Sausage on Polenta Verdura

We tend to pass up pork sausage in favor of the less fatty turkey or chicken sausage so popular today. Since meat processors have become keenly aware of America's growing health consciousness, even sausage has become leaner, and as we've mentioned before, pork itself is not the fatty meat it once was. So we've included this tasty main dish because a well-seasoned pork sausage can't be beat and because "not often" makes us toe the mark better than "never." Besides, we don't need a whole platter of them to make us purr. If you're going to indulge, do search out a good Italian market that sells homemade sausage. Mass-produced, packaged sausage never quite measures up.

Serves 4

1 cup imported instant polenta
1 can (14½ ounces) low-sodium chicken broth
½ cup grated Parmigiano-Reggiano cheese
1 tablespoon extra-virgin olive oil
salt and freshly ground black pepper to taste
cornmeal
variety of vegetables for grilling: eggplant, onion, bell peppers,
    zucchini, plum tomatoes, cremini or portobello mushrooms
5 Italian sausages, mild or hot

Prepare the polenta according to the package instructions for firm polenta, using the chicken broth for part of the water. When the polenta is ready, stir in the cheese, olive oil, and salt and pepper. Turn it out into an oiled loaf pan and refrigerate until firm, at least 3 hours or overnight. Cut the loaf into 1-inch-thick slices and then diagonally into triangles. Dust them lightly with cornmeal.

Prepare the vegetables for the grill. Peel and slice eggplant and onion 1 inch thick. Stem and seed mixed colors of bell peppers and cut them where the ribs are marked. Cut zucchini in half lengthwise. Stem plum tomatoes and cut in half lengthwise. Stem and wipe off mushrooms. Leave cremini mushrooms whole and cut portobellos into wide strips. Spray all the vegetables with olive oil or rub over them lightly with oiled hands. Season them with salt and pepper.

If you're grilling indoors, preheat the oven to 200° and have an ovenproof platter next to the grill so you can keep everything warm while you work in relays. Outdoors, you can keep the platter warm off to the side of the grill. Grill all the vegetables first, starting with the onions, which should be almost soft before you add the eggplant and peppers. The tomatoes, zucchini, and mushrooms go on last. Everything should show some char or grid marks, and you don't need to peel the peppers or the tomatoes. Keep the vegetables warm while you cook the polenta and sausages. They should be ready in about 10 minutes, when they're handsomely striped with grid marks.

Cut the sausages into thick diagonal slices and arrange them over the vegetables. Stand the polenta, points up, around the edge of the platter.

Buon appetito!

● **nutritional breakdown (per serving)**

Calories: 614	Carbohydrates: 48 g	Protein: 28 g	Fat: 34 g
Saturated fat: 11 g	% calories from fat: 50%	Cholesterol: 75 mg	Sodium: 1,116 mg

Ham Steak with Peach Chutney

These days we can find fresh peaches in the dead of winter, and they make a perfectly wonderful chutney even when the fruit isn't seasonally ripe. As for a nice thick ham steak, it develops personality when it's grilled, particularly over charcoal. Try precooking lengthwise-quartered sweet potatoes until not quite soft. Dip them in butter melted with curry powder and put them on the grill with the ham. A side dish of creamy coleslaw would be a worthy accompaniment.

Serves 4

Peach Chutney:

1½ cups chopped peeled peaches, with the juice

¼ teaspoon ground coriander

1 teaspoon grated lime zest

¼ teaspoon freshly grated nutmeg

⅛ teaspoon ground cloves

pinch of salt

¼ cup currants, raisins, or sweetened dried cranberries

1 tablespoon snipped fresh chives

½ teaspoon Caribbean-style hot sauce

3 tablespoons peach jam

1 tablespoon rice or champagne vinegar

1-pound ham steak, 1 inch thick

Put all the ingredients for the chutney in a covered microwave-proof dish and cook on high for 5 minutes. Drain the peaches with a slotted spoon, pressing them gently so their juices run back into the dish. Set the peaches aside in a storage container.

Return the liquid to the microwave and reduce it on high in 2- to 3-minute intervals, or until syrupy and thickened. Pour it back over the peaches and store in the refrigerator. The chutney will taste best if the flavors are allowed to develop at least overnight. It will keep more than a week in an airtight container.

Grill the ham steak indoors or out for 5 minutes on each side. Serve with the chutney.

nutritional breakdown (per serving)

Calories: 225	Carbohydrates: 30 g	Protein: 20 g	Fat: 4 g
Saturated fat: 1 g	% calories from fat: 16%	Cholesterol: 53 mg	Sodium: 1,420 mg

Peppered Buffalo Steak

Whoa-a! A Hollywood vision of buffalo herds stampeding over the Great Plains doesn't exactly awaken the appetite, nor does the thought of grilling a two-thousand-pound beast. Forget all that. Raising buffalo is a rapidly rising enterprise for small-herd western ranchers, who are slowly marketing the packaged meat as a low-cholesterol, low-fat, amazingly delicious alternative to beef. It's appealing to note that, unlike industry-raised cattle, buffalo are not fed either antibiotics or steroids. Take our word for it, buffalo burgers (page 174) and the tender rib-eye steaks grilled here taste more like beef than beef itself. We've tried to prove our point by preparing an American version of the classic French *steak au poivre*. It is not, however, for the well-done-meat lover. The lean quality of buffalo steak requires quick cooking over high heat and only to the rare stage.

Serves 4

2 tablespoons mixed whole peppercorns
2 buffalo rib-eye steaks
coarse salt to taste
1 tablespoon unsalted butter
¼ cup minced red onion
⅓ cup bourbon
⅓ cup canned low-sodium beef broth
pinch of salt
3 tablespoons heavy cream

Coarsely grind the peppercorns in a spice mill or crack them in a plastic bag with a mallet or hammer. Be careful not to leave any whole ones—they're nasty if you bite into one. Press the pepper into the steak on both sides. It should cover the meat entirely. Despite your fears, this isn't too much. Season the steaks with coarse salt.

Melt the butter in a small skillet and sauté the onion until very soft and slightly golden. Add the bourbon and let it sizzle a few seconds to burn off the alcohol. Add the beef broth and reduce the liquid by half. Add a pinch of salt.

Grill the steaks over high heat on either an indoor or outdoor grill for 2 to 3 minutes per side. If using a lidded electric grill, cook only 4 minutes altogether. Be watchful that the meat remains quite rare or it will become unpleasantly dry.

While the steak is grilling, add the cream to the bourbon sauce and reduce it over medium-high heat until it thickens slightly. Serve the steak in thin overlapping slices and nap the slices with the sauce. Serve immediately.

nutritional breakdown (per serving)

Calories: 277	Carbohydrates: 3 g	Protein: 37 g	Fat: 10 g
Saturated fat: 6 g	% calories from fat: 34%	Cholesterol: 128 mg	Sodium: 357 mg

Rabbit with Vidalia Onion Mustard Sauce

As the French have known for centuries, rabbit is perfectly delicious, much like chicken in taste but sweeter; the texture is closer to that of veal. The rabbit being farmed and marketed in some supermarkets and specialty food stores today is a younger, more tender creature than its wild or backyard-hutch cousins, which are best used in weekend stews. The smaller commercial rabbit takes well to the outdoor grill or the large basket of a rotisserie. There's only one problem, other than the fact that it's pricey. When you unfurl it from its vacuum-sealed packaging, it looks like a stretch limo in animal form. Prevail on the butcher to cut it up for you and crack the backbone to flatten it. The only meat worth grilling is on the saddle and the back legs—save the front end for the stockpot.

Serves 4

1 rabbit cut up, about 4 pounds
2 tablespoons extra-virgin olive oil
1 tablespoon Dijon mustard
salt and freshly ground black pepper to taste

Sauce:
2 strips smoky bacon
1 Vidalia or other sweet onion, chopped
3 garlic cloves, smashed and minced
pinch of cayenne
salt and freshly ground black pepper to taste
8 fresh sage leaves, stacked and cut in thin ribbons

3 tablespoons honey mustard
1¼ cups dry white wine
¼ cup orange juice

Rinse the rabbit pieces and dry completely. Whisk together the oil and mustard and rub the mixture on the rabbit. Season with salt and pepper. Put the pieces in a large rotisserie basket and set the timer for 45 minutes. Or sear the rabbit over a medium-hot fire on an outdoor grill and continue cooking for another 30 minutes.

Meanwhile, make the sauce. Crisp the bacon in a skillet and remove to a paper towel to drain. When cooled, crumble the bacon and set aside. Pour off all but 1 tablespoon of fat from the skillet and add the onion; sauté until golden. Add the garlic, cayenne, salt and pepper, and sage. Cover the skillet and lower the heat. When the mixture is soft, whisk in the mustard.

Reduce the wine and orange juice by almost half, either in the microwave on high for 4 to 5 minutes or on the stovetop over medium-high heat. Whisk the liquid into the onion-mustard mixture and cook until it thickens to a velvety pouring consistency. Taste for seasoning and adjust, if necessary.

Pour the sauce over the rabbit, and garnish with the crumbled bacon.

● **nutritional breakdown (per serving)**

Calories: 455	Carbohydrates: 17 g	Protein: 39 g	Fat: 25 g
Saturated fat: 6 g	% calories from fat: 49%	Cholesterol: 110 mg	Sodium: 643 mg

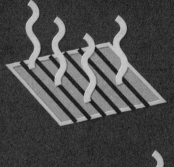

Poultry

Padre Island Chicken with Tomatillo Salsa

Pollo Diavolo

Chicken Beirut

Spicy Lime and Cilantro Chicken

Lemon Chicken Kabobs with Tomato Marmalade

Herb- and Parmesan-Crusted Chicken Breasts

Chicken Breasts with Peppered Chèvre and Olives

Chicken Breasts Filled with Peanut Sauce

Moroccan Cornish Hen

Ponzu Cornish Hen with Shiitake

Ginger Honey Duck

Duck Out of Africa

Glazed Black Duck

Smoky Maple Rum Turkey

Padre Island Chicken with Tomatillo Salsa

The salsa is the star of this terrific chicken dish, and we're willing to bet you'll make it often. It would be as welcome over any fish fillet and makes a sprightly change from the usual dip for tortilla chips. Chicken thighs and wings are a richer counterpoint to this light no-fat salsa, but you could use chicken breasts for an even lighter version. Either way, serve the dish with soft corn tortillas and a tossed green salad—preferably with avocado, slivered scallions, and grape tomatoes.

Serves 4

4 chicken thighs, with or without skin, preferably bone-in
12 chicken wings, tips removed
chili powder and salt to taste
canola oil

Salsa:
6 tomatillos, husked, stemmed, and chopped
2 serrano peppers, stemmed and seeded
6 scallions, trimmed and chopped
3 garlic cloves, chopped
¼ cup fresh cilantro leaves and tender stems
¼ teaspoon salt
½ teaspoon sugar

Rub all the chicken pieces liberally with chili powder and salt. If you're using skinless chicken, rub the pieces first with canola oil. Set aside for at least 30 minutes.

Combine all the salsa ingredients in a food processor until finely chopped but not pureed. Loosen the mixture with water as you pulse the processor. Taste for seasoning and adjust. After standing a while, the salsa may become watery, in which case simply drain off a little to regain the right consistency. Not too much flavor will be lost. This is meant to be a loose mixture.

If you're grilling bone-in thighs over white-ash charcoal, lid down, the juices should run clear in about 10 minutes. Boneless meat and wings will take a couple of minutes less. Just be certain there is no trace of pink in the juice.

If you're using an indoor electric grill with a lid, 5 minutes should be enough—a couple of minutes less for boneless, skinless thighs or wings.

Spoon salsa over chicken and serve.

cook's note: For a splendid shrimp dip, drain off most of the liquid from the salsa, add more zip with a few dashes of bottled hot sauce, and stir in just enough light sour cream to prevent the salsa from dripping.

When you make this recipe, buy and grill a couple of extra boneless thighs. We produced a delicious leftover we like to call Tex-Mex Scrapple, although, happily, the similarity to traditional scrapple ends with its appearance. Finely chop the meat, butter a standard loaf pan, and set both aside. Make 4 servings of instant polenta according to the instructions on the box, using canned low-salt chicken broth instead of water. When the polenta is soft and ready to be turned out, add 1 cup of grated Fontina or Monterey Jack cheese, a big knob of butter, salt and pepper, and the finely chopped chicken. Pack it into the loaf pan and refrigerate until firm, or overnight. Cut the loaf into 1-inch-thick slices and coat them lightly with cornmeal. Grill indoors or out until hot and handsomely striped with golden brown. Serve with a zesty prepared or homemade salsa and a dollop of light sour cream

nutritional breakdown (per serving)

Calories: 484	Carbohydrates: 7 g	Protein: 44 g	Fat: 30 g
Saturated fat: 8 g	% calories from fat: 56%	Cholesterol: 143 mg	Sodium: 447 mg

(without skin)

Calories: 439	Carbohydrates: 7 g	Protein: 42 g	Fat: 26 g
Saturated fat: 7 g	% calories from fat: 53%	Cholesterol: 135 mg	Sodium: 441 mg

Pollo Diavolo

Somewhere between a Tuscan trattoria and El Pollo Loco lies proof that the simplest recipes are always the best. Anoint a plump chicken with a singular olive oil, aromatic herbs, a lick of garlic, the kick of pepper, and lemon's welcome pucker, and that's about as good as it gets. That is, of course, if you grill it expertly.

Serves 4

1 chicken, about 4 pounds
¼ cup extra-virgin olive oil
1½ teaspoons dried red pepper flakes
4 garlic cloves, smashed and minced
1 teaspoon grated lemon zest
1 tablespoon coarse salt
1 tablespoon chopped fresh oregano
1 tablespoon fresh thyme leaves
paper-thin lemon slices, as needed

Remove the parts stored in the cavity of the chicken. Cut off the wingtips and tail. Place the chicken breast side down and use poultry shears or a heavy knife to cut down each side of the backbone and remove it. Turn the bird over and flatten it by striking a few deft blows with a mallet or meat pounder. Rinse the chicken and pat dry.

Heat the oil with the red pepper flakes and garlic just to the point of a simmer. Remove from the heat and allow to cool. Strain out the garlic and pepper flakes and add the lemon zest, salt, and herbs. Loosen the skin over the breast and thighs with your fingertips, pulling away any restraining membrane. Push the herb-zest mixture under the skin, reserving enough of the oil to thoroughly coat the outside of the bird. If there isn't enough, use a little more olive oil. Slide the lemon slices under the skin and pull the skin back into place. Cut 2 slits in the skin near the tail and anchor the drumsticks. Twist the wings back under the breast.

Sear the chicken, flesh side down first, over a hot fire to form a golden crust, 2 to 3 minutes per side. Move the chicken over to low or indirect heat and grill for another 15 minutes, or until the juices run clear and an instant-read thermometer registers 140° when inserted in the thickest part of the thigh. Baste with additional oil if the chicken starts looking dry.

cook's note: To achieve a perfectly cooked chicken over an outdoor fire requires some skill and a watchful eye to avoid charring the skin before the meat is thoroughly cooked. It's important to have two zones of heat so you can move the chicken back and forth when there are flare-ups and avoid turning the meat to Styrofoam over too high a flame. For that reason, only thermostatically controlled indoor grills will do a satisfactory job with a bone-in chicken. This recipe can be well prepared indoors, however, if you select boneless chicken parts with the skin left on.

● **nutritional breakdown (per serving)**

Calories: 442	Carbohydrates: 2 g	Protein: 36 g	Fat: 31 g
Saturated fat: 7 g	% calories from fat: 64%	Cholesterol: 144 mg	Sodium: 398 mg

● **(without skin)**

Calories: 344	Carbohydrates: 2 g	Protein: 33 g	Fat: 22 g
Saturated fat: 4 g	% calories from fat: 57%	Cholesterol: 101 mg	Sodium: 389 mg

Chicken Beirut

Sweet and hot peppers, garlic, cumin, pomegranates, and the aroma of hardwood charcoal are all reminiscent of Middle Eastern cuisine. Pomegranate syrup or molasses may seem a bit esoteric and the quantity required too small to bother with, but its mysterious addictive quality may have you reaching for it more often than you think. Easily attained in Middle Eastern markets, it's popping up in specialty food stores as well. We even found a pomegranate glazing sauce, under a popular Greek label, in a supermarket. Serve this tasty chicken with a cucumber, mint, and yogurt salad and a basket of toasted pita bread.

Serves 4

8 preferred chicken parts, bone-in for outdoor grilling, boneless for indoor grilling
salt and freshly ground black pepper to taste

Marinade:

4 garlic cloves, smashed
½ teaspoon ground cumin
2 large grilled, canned, or bottled roasted red peppers
3 red jalapeño or other hot red peppers, roasted and seeded
2 tablespoons extra-virgin olive oil
1 teaspoon salt
1 tablespoon pomegranate syrup or molasses (or 1 tablespoon lemon juice + 1 teaspoon honey)

Rinse the chicken, pat dry, and season lightly with salt and pepper. Drop the parts into a plastic bag.

Put the ingredients for the marinade in a food processor and puree. Pour over the chicken, seal the bag tightly, and marinate for at least 2 hours. Remove the chicken from the bag and save the marinade.

Grill the chicken over hot coals to sear the flesh and crisp the skin for about 5 minutes. Move the parts to indirect heat and cook for another 15 minutes, or until the juices run clear. Baste with the reserved marinade as needed to form an even crust.

Cook boneless parts on a stovetop or electric grill for about 5 minutes per side. If using a lidded grill with the top down, cook for 4 to 5 minutes altogether.

nutritional breakdown (per serving)

Calories: 392	Carbohydrates: 4 g	Protein: 45 g	Fat: 21 g
Saturated fat: 5 g	% calories from fat: 47%	Cholesterol: 141 mg	Sodium: 449 mg

(without skin)

Calories: 296	Carbohydrates: 4 g	Protein: 41 g	Fat: 12 g
Saturated fat: 3 g	% calories from fat: 37%	Cholesterol: 123 mg	Sodium: 437 mg

Spicy Lime and Cilantro Chicken

C hicken is so adaptable it can take on any ethnic guise successfully. This one is almost Mexican and could drop even farther south if accompanied by a rice pilaf laced with fresh corn and a sparkling salad of sliced jicama, avocado, and oranges.

Serves 4

1 chicken, about 4 pounds

Seasoning Paste:
4 garlic cloves, smashed
1 large shallot, chopped
4 serrano peppers, stemmed and seeded
1 teaspoon ground white pepper
2 teaspoons coarse salt
½ teaspoon dried oregano, preferably Mexican
grated zest of 1 lime
½ cup chopped fresh cilantro

Basting Sauce:
4 tablespoons unsalted butter
juice of 1 lime
¼ cup chopped fresh cilantro
green chili hot sauce, optional (see Cook's Note)

R emove the parts from the cavity of the chicken and cut off any excess skin flaps, fat, and wing tips. Rinse the bird thoroughly and pat dry.

Combine the ingredients for the seasoning paste in a food processor. Release the skin of the chicken with your fingertips, tearing the connective membranes as needed. Be sure to wiggle your way over the thighs, which is about as far as you can go without risk of tearing the skin. Spread the paste under the skin as evenly as possible. Wash your hands carefully with soap and hot water when you're finished and remember not to touch your face; the hot chilies can give you a nasty burn. Truss the chicken by tying the legs together and tying the wings up close to the body.

Melt the butter in a small saucepan or a microwave-safe dish and add the rest of the basting ingredients. Stir to combine. Set aside with a basting brush.

Fit the chicken onto the spit of a rotisserie according to the manufacturer's directions and set the timer for 1 hour. Wash your hands again. Baste the bird lightly with the butter mixture and start the motor. After 30 minutes, baste every 10 minutes. The chicken will be done when the juices run clear or an instant-read thermometer inserted between the thigh and the body registers 165°.

cook's note: There are many green hot sauces on the market, including green Tabasco. Pick one for your pantry, as there are times, like this one, when you won't want red to muddy up your seasoning.

● **nutritional breakdown (per serving)**

Calories: 461	Carbohydrates: 5 g	Protein: 39 g	Fat: 31 g
Saturated fat: 13 g	% calories from fat: 60%	Cholesterol: 184 mg	Sodium: 827 mg

● **(without skin)**

Calories: 359	Carbohydrates: 5 g	Protein: 36 g	Fat: 21 g
Saturated fat: 10 g	% calories from fat: 53%	Cholesterol: 140 mg	Sodium: 819 mg

Lemon Chicken Kabobs with Tomato Marmalade

We love the brilliant red dash of this marmalade and the way these sparkling citrus and tomato flavors complement grilled chicken. The acidity of the marmalade is smoothed by the addition of pureed roasted red pepper, and dried red pepper flakes provide the zip. This marmalade makes a wonderful pizza topping in lieu of the usual tomato sauce—particularly with grilled eggplant—and it's also a good dip for vegetables. Double the recipe and refrigerate it for other uses. It keeps well for several days. These kabobs would taste terrific with rosemary hash brown potatoes.

Serves 4

3 boneless, skinless chicken breasts
3 boneless, skinless chicken thighs
grated zest and juice of 1 lemon, or 8 drops pure lemon oil
extra-virgin olive oil
salt and freshly ground black pepper to taste

Marmalade:
6 plum tomatoes, stemmed
3 garlic cloves, smashed and minced
¼ teaspoon dried red pepper flakes
salt to taste
½ teaspoon sugar
1 cup loosely packed flat-leaf parsley
1 teaspoon tomato paste
1 tablespoon fresh lemon juice
½ cup jarred roasted red peppers, drained

Pull off the long, slender chicken tender that lies along the underside of the breast. Store them in the freezer for future stir-fries. Flatten out the thickest part of the breast with a mallet or the side of a heavy cleaver. Cut each half into wide lengthwise ribbons for easy threading on skewers. Cut the thighs into large chunks. Marinate the chicken in the lemon zest and juice for 30 minutes; drain and rub lightly with olive oil. (If using the pure lemon oil, mix it with ¼ cup olive oil and coat the chicken at least 30 minutes before grilling.) Season the chicken with salt and pepper.

Put the tomatoes, garlic, red pepper flakes, salt, and sugar in a flat microwave-safe dish in one layer. Cook on high for 10 minutes. Turn the tomatoes over, lifting off the skin and removing any visible clumps of seeds or white pulp. If any liquid remains, cook for another 3 minutes on high.

Transfer the tomatoes to a food processor, add the rest of the marmalade ingredients, and pulse to make a thick, fluid sauce. Taste for seasoning and adjust.

Thread the flat chicken breast strips, ribbon candy fashion, onto water-soaked wooden skewers or onto the metal ones that fit into a rotisserie. Thread the thigh meat securely, either separately or alternately. Grill the kabobs on a rotisserie for about 20 minutes, or until all juices run clear. Grill them on a lidded electric grill for about 5 minutes and outdoors over white-ash coals about 3 minutes per side.

Warm the tomato marmalade slightly and place the kabobs over a splash of it on the plate. Serve additional marmalade separately.

nutritional breakdown (per serving)

| Calories: 242 | Carbohydrates: 8 g | Protein: 31 g | Fat: 9 g |
| Saturated fat: 2 g | % calories from fat: 33% | Cholesterol: 92 mg | Sodium: 297 mg |

Herb- and Parmesan-Crusted Chicken Breasts

This is an intensely flavorful, crispy chicken dish that retains as much of the natural juices as possible without being sautéed in oil. The trick is to refrigerate the breasts for at least an hour before grilling to set and dry the coating. The Japanese bread crumbs called *panko* make an amazing difference to the crunch, so it's worth searching them out. They come in plastic bags packed by Wel-Pac and are increasingly available in fine supermarkets and specialty food stores. These chicken cutlets would pair splendidly with a grilled eggplant and potato gratin and a simple tossed green salad.

Serves 4

4 boneless, skinless chicken breast halves
2 tablespoons each minced fresh thyme, sage, chives, and flat-leaf parsley
¾ cup panko bread crumbs or lightly toasted fine fresh crumbs
¼ cup grated Parmesan cheese
salt and freshly ground black pepper to taste
1 tablespoon extra-virgin olive oil
2 egg whites, lightly beaten

Pull off the long, slender chicken tender that lies along the underside of the breast. Store them in the freezer for future stir-fries. Slightly flatten the thickest part of the meat with a mallet or the back of a heavy cleaver.

Combine the herbs, bread crumbs, grated cheese, and salt and pepper. Slowly drizzle the olive oil over the mixture, lightly working it into the crumbs with your fingertips, keeping the mixture loose and fluffy. Spread the coating out on a cookie sheet.

Dip the chicken breasts into the egg white. Drain off the excess. Firmly press each cutlet into the coating to cover it thoroughly. Lay the chicken on a wax-paper-lined plate and refrigerate, uncovered, for at least an hour.

Cook the chicken breasts on a stovetop or lidded electric grill for about 3 minutes per side or 4 to 5 minutes with the lid down. Or grill over white-ash coals outdoors, about 3 minutes per side, or until the juices run clear.

nutritional breakdown (per serving)

Calories: 293	Carbohydrates: 9 g	Protein: 41 g	Fat: 9 g
Saturated fat: 3 g	% calories from fat: 28%	Cholesterol: 100 mg	Sodium: 382 mg

Chicken Breasts with Peppered Chèvre and Olives

A flavorful stuffing for boneless grilled chicken breasts keeps them moist over intense heat and rescues them from the terminal blahs. The same filling can be inserted into a pocket, following the procedure for Chicken Breasts Filled with Peanut Sauce on page 92, but this is a less fussy preparation and the attractive presentation suits the creamy ingredients. We can think of several other "sandwich" fillings that you might want to try, such as mango chutney mixed with low-fat cream cheese or a simple spread of pesto or olivada.

Serves 4

4 boneless, skinless chicken breast halves
1 peppered chèvre cheese button, 3 ounces
2 tablespoons minced fresh chives
12 pitted Kalamata olives, chopped
2 teaspoons roasted garlic (see box on page 127)
pinch of salt
extra-virgin olive oil

Pull off the long, slender chicken tender that lies along the underside of the breast. Store them in the freezer for future stir-fries. Lay the breasts on a cutting board, smooth side up. Flatten them with a mallet or the back of a heavy cleaver, just to even out the thickness of the meat.

Mash together the cheese, chives, olives, garlic, and salt to make a smooth paste. Spread a layer ⅛ inch thick over 2 breast halves, leaving a ½-inch margin around the edges.

Sandwich the breasts with the remaining 2 halves and press down firmly to seal.

Rub the surface of the chicken with the olive oil to prevent sticking.

In a lidded electric grill, the chicken breasts will be done in less than 5 minutes. Test to be certain the flesh is opaque throughout. On an outdoor grill over white-ash coals, they should take about 3 minutes per side.

Slice the breasts thickly on the diagonal and serve immediately.

cook's note: If there is any filling left over, save it for spreading on crackers.

● **nutritional breakdown (per serving)**

Calories: 273	Carbohydrates: 2 g	Protein: 38 g	Fat: 12 g
Saturated fat: 4 g	% calories from fat: 38%	Cholesterol: 103 mg	Sodium: 271 mg

Chicken Breasts Filled with Peanut Sauce

This is a simple all-American spin on Indonesian satay, made with familiar ingredients already in your cupboard. It's a delicious dress-up for the modest chicken breast, and the method of putting the flavor in the pocket should inspire many creative variations. This version would pair well with a sprightly white fried rice with petite peas, slivered carrot, scallions, and broccoli florets, made without the usual dousing of soy sauce.

Serves 4

4 boneless, skinless chicken breast halves

Sauce:

3 tablespoons smooth peanut butter

1 tablespoon ketchup

1 teaspoon Worcestershire sauce

1 tablespoon honey

1 teaspoon red wine vinegar

3 garlic cloves, smashed and minced

2 tablespoons minced fresh chives

½ teaspoon salt

¼ teaspoon cayenne, or to taste

peanut or canola oil

finely ground dry-roasted peanuts for garnish, optional

minced fresh cilantro for garnish, optional

Pull off the long, slender chicken tenders that lie along the underside of the breasts. Store them in the freezer for future stir-fries. Lay the breasts on a cutting board, smooth side up. Starting at the middle of the rounded end and using a sharp, thin utility knife, slit a wide pocket all the way around to within an inch of the thin tip. Follow the contours of the chicken breast and don't worry if your opening is a couple of inches wide—the filling won't ooze out.

Combine the sauce ingredients in a food processor. Taste for seasoning and adjust. The sauce should be only slightly sweet but very piquant. Push the sauce into the pocket with your fingers, covering as much of the interior surface as possible. Lightly coat the outside of the breasts with oil to prevent sticking.

In a lidded electric grill, the chicken breasts will be done in less than 5 minutes. Test to be certain the flesh is opaque throughout. On an outdoor grill over white-ash coals, they should take about 3 minutes per side. Serve immediately with a dusting of ground peanuts and minced cilantro.

cook's note: Save any excess peanut sauce to spread on rice crackers for a dandy snack.

● **nutritional breakdown (per serving)**

Calories: 298	Carbohydrates: 9 g	Protein: 38 g	Fat: 12 g
Saturated fat: 3 g	% calories from fat: 36%	Cholesterol: 96 mg	Sodium: 495 mg

Moroccan Cornish Hen

Sadly, the Cornish hen always seems the little orphan of the poultry display case. Now that they have been bred into more zaftig creatures, they are no longer scrawny single servings leaving a plateful of messy bones. One hen is now sufficient for two. They are perfect cooked whole on the rotisserie, and when split—with the backbone removed—they grill quickly and attractively both indoors or out.

The yogurt marinade keeps the tender meat moist, and the unusual spice combination provides a haunting flavor. Serve these exotic birds with couscous tossed with currants.

Serves 4

2 Cornish hens

Marinade:
2 cups plain nonfat yogurt
6 garlic cloves, smashed and minced
8 large scallions minced, with 1½ inches of the green
1 teaspoon ground cumin
1 teaspoon turmeric
½ teaspoon ground allspice
2 teaspoons hot Hungarian or Spanish paprika
2 teaspoons coarse salt
2 tablespoons canola oil

1 cup ground blanched almonds or pistachios (available unsalted in Middle Eastern markets)

Rinse and clean the hens, patting them dry with paper towels inside and out. Put each one in a plastic bag. In a medium mixing bowl, combine the marinade ingredients thoroughly and add half of the marinade to each hen. Twist each bag closed and squeeze the marinade around the hen to coat it completely. Leave the hens to marinate in the refrigerator for at least 2 to 3 hours, preferably overnight.

Remove the hens from their bags and discard the excess marinade. Dust the hens with the nuts and secure them to the spit of an electric rotisserie. Roast for about 45 minutes, or until an instant-read thermometer registers 170° at the base of the thigh. If you don't have a meat thermometer, test to be certain the juices run clear.

cook's note: Should you prefer grilling the hens on an outside barbecue, follow the instructions for splitting and cooking them on page 96 (Ponzu Cornish Hen with Shiitake).

● **nutritional breakdown (per serving)**

| Calories: 573 | Carbohydrates: 11 g | Protein: 38 g | Fat: 42 g |
| Saturated fat: 8 g | % calories from fat: 66% | Cholesterol: 169 mg | Sodium: 308 mg |

● **(without skin)**

| Calories: 387 | Carbohydrates: 11 g | Protein: 35 g | Fat: 23 g |
| Saturated fat: 3 g | % calories from fat: 53% | Cholesterol: 117 mg | Sodium: 295 mg |

Ponzu Cornish Hen
with Shiitake

Ponzu is a tangy citrus-based sauce used frequently in Japanese cooking. It contains such exotica as kelp and bonito flakes, but if you can't find it already prepared and bottled in the Asian section of your supermarket or a specialty food store, you can approximate the flavor by combining ½ cup lemon juice with 2 tablespoons each rice vinegar and mirin and ⅓ cup soy sauce. Add the punch of 2 or 3 crushed slices of fresh ginger.

Like most traditional Japanese dishes, this one is spare, restrained, and totally refreshing. The sweet, elegant, little Cornish hen seems born for these precise flavors.

Serves 2

1 Cornish hen, 1½ to 1¾ pounds
5 to 6 ounces shiitake mushrooms, stemmed down to the cap
2 bunches slender scallions, trimmed and slivered
salt and freshly ground black pepper to taste
cold-pressed pure peanut oil, sometimes marked "fragrant"
1 bottle prepared ponzu sauce
1 tablespoon wasabi powder

Turn the hen, breast side down, on a cutting board. With a pair of poultry shears or sturdy kitchen scissors, cut along both sides of the backbone to reveal the cavity. Discard the backbone. Snip off any excess gobs of fat on skin flaps. Cut the hen in half as close as possible to both sides of the breastbone, releasing the ribs. Discard the breastbone. You can also cut away the small rib bones if you like. Rinse the 2 halves and pat dry. Cut 2 slits in the skin near the tail and slip in the tip of the drumstick so the bird lies flat. Fold the wingtips back and under the breast.

Slice 4 of the shiitake mushrooms very thinly. Combine them with some of the slivered scallions, season with salt and pepper, and drizzle with enough peanut oil to coat.

Work your fingers under the skin of the hen all the way into the leg, as far as you can go without tearing it. Break any connective membrane as you go. This is easier than you might think. Push half of the mushroom mixture into each hen half, covering as much of the flesh as you can. Pull the skin back into place. Season the hen lightly with salt and pepper and drop the halves into a plastic bag. Pour in just enough ponzu sauce to cover sparingly and marinate for at least a couple of hours.

In a tiny dish, mix the wasabi powder with just enough water to make a firm paste. Roll it into tiny balls and place in a dish. Cover tightly with plastic wrap, and let it sit for at least 15 minutes to develop the flavor.

Remove the hen and discard the marinade. Rub the hen and the remaining mushrooms with peanut oil. Season with salt and pepper and place the mushrooms in a small metal basket if you're grilling outdoors. Cook the hen on a stovetop, electric, or medium-hot outdoor grill for about 8 minutes per side or in a large lidded electric grill for a total of about 12 minutes. In both cases, the leg will wiggle freely and the juices will run clear to signal doneness.

Grill the mushrooms briefly until just limp and tender. Mix them with the remaining scallion slivers. Serve the hen halves with the mushrooms and scallions on top. Serve individual dipping dishes of ponzu sauce and little balls of wasabi for the valiant.

● **nutritional breakdown (per serving)**

Calories: 569	Carbohydrates: 26 g	Protein: 33 g	Fat: 37 g
Saturated fat: 9 g	% calories from fat: 58%	Cholesterol: 168 mg	Sodium: 1,793 mg

● **(without skin)**

Calories: 382	Carbohydrates: 26 g	Protein: 30 g	Fat: 18 g
Saturated fat: 3 g	% calories from fat: 42%	Cholesterol: 117 mg	Sodium: 1,780 mg

Ginger Honey Duck

The sweet and spicy seasoning so frequently used in Asian cooking seems a natural foil for the rich meat of duck. This treatment almost reaches the height of the revered Peking duck, and you don't have to fuss around with all those fragile pancakes to enjoy it. If you want blissful sighs from your guests, serve this lovely spit-roasted bird with a bountiful platter of rice noodles in a coconut curry sauce, garnished with cilantro.

Serves 2

1 duck, about 5 pounds

Marinade:

½ cup soy sauce

¼ cup sherry vinegar

6 quarter-size coins fresh ginger, peeled, smashed, and slivered

4 garlic cloves, smashed and chopped

Basting Sauce

¼ cup soy sauce

2 tablespoons honey

2 tablespoons ginger marmalade, British import label

2 teaspoons frozen orange juice concentrate

2 teaspoons fresh lemon juice

1 tablespoon hoisin sauce

2 teaspoons Chinese five-spice powder

Trim the duck breasts of any excess skin flaps or exterior fat. Pinch the skin between thumb and forefinger and, using sharp, pointed scissors, snip several little sideways V-shaped cuts in the skin, just through to the fat. Don't pierce the flesh. This will allow the fat to run free as it melts.

Combine all the ingredients for the marinade. Put the duck and the marinade in a large plastic bag, seal it tightly, and refrigerate overnight.

Remove the duck and the marinade to a large rectangular microwave-safe dish. Add ½ cup water, tent the duck completely with a paper towel, and precook it on high for 10 minutes. A great deal of the surface fat will drain into the dish. Remove the duck and pat it dry. Refrigerate, uncovered, for at least 2 to 3 hours. This will dry the skin and help to keep it crisp.

Combine the basting sauce ingredients in a small dish and heat in the microwave to melt the honey and marmalade. The sauce should be thick and syrupy in about 3 minutes on high. Stand a basting brush in the sauce to moisten it and set aside.

Truss the bird by tying the legs together and the wings up close to the body. You may need another cross tie somewhere south of the midsection to keep the package compact. Insert the duck on the spit of a rotisserie according to the manufacturer's directions and set the timer for 30 minutes. Baste the duck at the beginning and, after fifteen minutes, baste it often until it has a deep brown, crusty glaze.

Warm any remaining basting sauce, carve the duck, and drizzle a little sauce over each serving.

● **nutritional breakdown (per serving)**

Calories: 745	Carbohydrates: 41 g	Protein: 37 g	Fat: 49 g
Saturated fat: 17 g	% calories from fat: 58%	Cholesterol: 143 mg	Sodium: 2,653 mg

● **(without skin)**

Calories: 457	Carbohydrates: 41 g	Protein: 37 g	Fat: 16 g
Saturated fat: 6 g	% calories from fat: 32%	Cholesterol: 126 mg	Sodium: 2,645 mg

Duck Out of Africa

This is how we imagine an African safari chef might prepare duck breasts over his campfire. The exotic contrast of flavors is as delicious as the imaginings, and the subtle infusion of hardwood smoke merely gilds the duck, so to speak. You can easily adapt this recipe to a whole duck for the rotisserie or halves or quarters for the grill. You can also adjust ingredient quantities to the number of servings. To complete the meal, alternate the papaya with grilled parsnips and green bell pepper strips and toss up a salad of mixed bitter greens.

Serves 2

1 whole boneless duck breast, split

Marinade:

1 tablespoon canola oil

¼ cup frozen orange juice concentrate

¼ cup fresh lime juice

1 tablespoon grated lime zest

1 habanero pepper, seeded and minced

1 tablespoon coarse salt

¼ teaspoon ground cloves

1 tablespoon light brown sugar

Garnish:

Sliced ripe papaya dipped in melted butter and grated nutmeg

Trim the duck breasts of any excess skin flaps or exterior fat. Pinch the skin between thumb and forefinger and, using sharp, pointed scissors, snip several little sideways V-shaped cuts in the skin, just through to the fat. Don't pierce the flesh. This will allow the fat to run free as it melts.

Combine the marinade ingredients in a glass measure or a microwave-safe dish and heat in the microwave on high until simmering, 1 to 1½ minutes. Stir to incorporate the melted sugar. Cool enough to taste and adjust the balance of flavors to your taste. If the marinade is too tart, you may need a tad more sugar; if it's too sweet, add more lime. If you'd like a stronger clove flavor you can add more with caution. Too much clove is overwhelming.

Tuck the duck breasts into a plastic bag and pour the marinade over them. Seal tightly and marinate for at least an hour.

Remove the duck brasts and reserve the remaining marinade. Grill the duck, skin side down, on a hot stovetop, electric, or medium-hot charcoal grill for about 3 minutes. Turn the breasts, flesh side down, and cook for another 2 to 3 minutes for a perfect pink interior. If you're using a lidded electric grill, lay the lid out flat and cook the duck one side at a time as instructed above. Lay the papaya slices on the grill during the last 2 minutes of cooking.

Quickly bring any remaining marinade to a boil. Slice the duck breasts thinly, fan the slices out on warm serving plates, and drizzle the marinade over them. Garnish with the papaya and serve immediately.

nutritional breakdown (per serving)

Calories: 398	Carbohydrates: 24 g	Protein: 31 g	Fat: 20 g
Saturated fat: 4 g	% calories from fat: 45%	Cholesterol: 163 mg	Sodium: 1,850 mg

(without skin)

Calories: 288	Carbohydrates: 24 g	Protein: 27 g	Fat: 9 g
Saturated fat: 1 g	% calories from fat: 29%	Cholesterol: 136 mg	Sodium: 1,849 mg

Glazed Black Duck

If you love duck in restaurants but recoil from cooking it at home, the grill and/or rotisserie is for you. The intense heat of the grill does an expert job of releasing the subcutaneous fat and crisping the skin, and the rotisserie does equally well with the whole bird. It was pure serendipity that turned this duck breast black. We simply lucked out. If you lust for duck but think of it only as a special-occasion dish, this recipe for two should convince you to experiment, even if you and your grill are home alone. Leftover duck makes great fried rice! To that end, serve this dish with more than enough steamed jasmine rice with petite peas and scallions.

Serves 2

1 whole boneless duck breast, split

Glazing Sauce:

3 tablespoons rice vinegar

2 tablespoons reduced-sodium Japanese soy sauce

2 tablespoons Chinese black soy sauce, or 2 tablespoons low-sodium soy + pinch of sugar

4 quarter-size slices fresh ginger, peeled, smashed and minced

½ teaspoon cracked black pepper

¼ teaspoon Chinese five-spice powder

¼ teaspoon ground coriander

½ teaspoon dried lavender, optional

¼ cup blackberry jelly or seedless jam

black sesame seeds, optional

Trim the duck breasts of any excess skin flaps or exterior fat. Pinch the skin between thumb and forefinger and, using sharp pointed scissors, snip several little sideways V-shaped cuts in the skin, just through to the fat. Don't pierce the flesh. This will allow the fat to run free as it melts.

Combine all the glaze ingredients except the jelly in a glass 2-cup measure or microwave-safe bowl in the microwave and cook on high for 1½ minutes. Let the sauce sit for a couple of minutes, then strain out the bits of ginger. Stir in the blackberry jelly and return to the microwave for 2½ minutes on high, or until the sauce is thickened and syrupy. Taste for seasoning and adjust. Soften a basting brush in the sauce and set aside

Grill the duck, skin side down, on a hot stovetop, electric, or medium-hot charcoal grill for about 3 minutes, glazing with the sauce at the halfway point. Turn the breasts, flesh side down, cook for another minute, glaze again, and finish cooking for another minute or two for a perfect pink interior. If you're using a lidded electric grill, lay the lid out flat and cook the duck one side at a time as instructed above.

Slice the duck on the diagonal and drizzle with the remaining hot sauce. Sprinkle with the black sesame seeds and serve immediately.

● **nutritional breakdown (per serving)**

Calories: 345	Carbohydrates: 23 g	Protein: 31 g	Fat: 13 g
Saturated fat: 4 g	% calories from fat: 34%	Cholesterol: 163 mg	Sodium: 1,009 mg

● **(without skin)**

Calories: 235	Carbohydrates: 23 g	Protein: 28 g	Fat: 2 g
Saturated fat: 1 g	% calories from fat: 9%	Cholesterol: 136 mg	Sodium: 1,008 mg

Smoky Maple Rum Turkey

It's really hard not to think of all the accoutrements of Thanksgiving when you cook a turkey, even though many of us have wondered why we don't enjoy our holiday bird more often. The little 10-pound and under teeny-bopper may not be as flavorful as the big old free-range Tom, but it still tastes like turkey and it's a joy to roast on the spit of a rotisserie. It would be even better in an outdoor smoker if you have the equipment and the time. This is not an indoor grill recipe, but if you're lacking a rotisserie, you can certainly roast this mini bird in the oven. The skin comes out with the glossy sheen of mahogany patent leather, so it's the perfect do-ahead centerpiece for a summer buffet.

Serves 10

1 small turkey, 10 pounds
salt and freshly ground black pepper to taste
2 tablespoons unsalted butter, at room temperature
1 tablespoon each minced fresh sage, thyme, and chives

Basting Sauce:

½ cup gold rum

1 tablespoon unsalted butter

4 garlic cloves, smashed

4 quarter-size coins fresh ginger, peeled and smashed

4 small dried red chilies, seeded and crushed, or 2 teaspoons dried red pepper flakes

6 whole cardamom pods

2 teaspoons salt

1½ teaspoons ground allspice

½ cup amber pure maple syrup, not maple-flavored syrup

3 tablespoons cider vinegar

2 tablespoons fresh lemon juice

2 teaspoons Worcestershire sauce

1 teaspoon liquid smoke, optional

Remove the turkey parts from the cavity, saving the neck for broth. Thoroughly rinse the turkey inside and out under cool running water and blot it completely dry with paper towels. Cut off the wingtips and tail. Sprinkle the outside of the bird with salt and pepper.

Combine the softened butter with the herbs and salt and pepper to make a thick green paste. Loosen the skin from the breast and thighs of the bird with your fingertips, tearing away any restraining membrane. Push the paste over the flesh, distributing it as deep into the carcass as you can. Fold up a piece of aluminum foil to just fit over the breast and tuck it down on both sides between the leg and breast. This will keep the breast from drying out before the legs are cooked.

Be sure the drumsticks are tucked into the tail-skin flap, and tie the bird securely with kitchen twine around the wings and the widest part of the thighs. Insert the turkey on the rotisserie spit, following the manufacturer's guidelines and making sure that the bird clears all sides of the rotisserie. You may have to reposition it a couple of times and/or adjust the trussing.

Combine the basting ingredients in a small saucepan and bring to a boil. Simmer slowly for about 15 minutes, or until the sauce is reduced to a thick, syrupy glaze. You can also do this in the microwave; it will take approximately 5 minutes on high. Lift out the pieces of garlic and ginger. Baste the turkey lightly at the beginning of the cooking time and wait 30 minutes before basting again at 10-minute intervals. Stop the spit rotation after 45 minutes and carefully pull out the aluminum foil from under the string. It will take only an hour and 45 minutes to reach 165° on an instant-read thermometer, and the temperature will rise another 5° during the 15-minute resting period. Leave the turkey in the rotisserie during the rest period.

cook's notes: This recipe can also be used for chicken, pork, or duck.

The drippings in the bottom of the rotisserie make an interesting sauce for the turkey. Put the drip pan over medium heat on the stovetop and add some canned chicken broth. Bring to a simmer and scrape up all those lovely black bits stuck to the pan. Taste. If you'd like a tart sauce to offset the sweetness of the glaze, add some cider vinegar or lemon juice. If you'd like a bit more zip, sprinkle in cayenne or any hot sauce to taste.

Thicken the sauce ever so slightly with a slurry of equal parts arrowroot and water. Don't use flour, even the shake-and-blend kind, which will make the glossy sauce cloudy. What you're striving for here is a natural gravy to add some moisture to the meat.

● **nutritional breakdown (per serving)**

Calories: 443	Carbohydrates: 8 g	Protein: 51 g	Fat: 21 g
Saturated fat: 7 g	% calories from fat: 42%	Cholesterol: 157 mg	Sodium: 707 mg

● **(without skin)**

Calories: 324	Carbohydrates: 8 g	Protein: 51 g	Fat: 8 g
Saturated fat: 4 g	% calories from fat: 21%	Cholesterol: 179 mg	Sodium: 699 mg

About Brining

The endless search for more and more flavor in our processed and farmed food has led chefs and cookbook authors to experiment with the ancient practice of brining—a simple method of preserving meat by soaking it in salt water. Preservation is no longer the issue, of course, but creative chefs have discovered that salted water carries flavor deep into meat and seems to intensify its natural flavor through a process of osmosis too convoluted to explain here. It also plumps the meat with moisture to the extent that it actually weighs more after brining and is juicier when cooked. We think success can be iffy for the novice because it's dependent upon the type and size of the meat, as well as the saltiness of the brining solution and the length of time the meat spends in it.

It all started with large turkeys, which seem to take to this procedure very well, but most of us have a hard enough time getting that big holiday bird in the refrigerator at all, let alone trying to cram it into a bucket of water. Whole chicken or bone-in parts and pork loin or chops offer less frustrating possibilities of success and a good place to begin this trial-and-error adventure. On page 111 is a basic formula you can play with.

For a 3- to 4-pound chicken,
8 bone-in chicken parts,
a whole pork loin,
or 6 1¼-inch-thick pork chops:

2 quarts hot water
½ cup coarse salt
⅓ cup sugar, honey, or maple syrup

Marinades

Marinating is a technique with a potentially serious impact on flavor. A purely oil-based marinade will lubricate the meat, but its seasoning won't penetrate far. An effective marinade needs the acidic quality of vinegar, citrus juice, white wine, tomato, soy sauce, or the penetrating enzymes in yogurt. Beer, cider, and various liquors also work. Think of seviche and how lime juice alone "cooks" the scallops. Think of how quickly a salad goes limp with too much vinegar in the dressing. Now, if it were made with lemon juice and you marinated chicken in it, you'd have a tart little chicken—boring, but tart. You can rely on the acidic content of the marinade to carry with it other add-in flavors and to tenderize tougher cuts of meat. A small amount of oil acts as an emulsifier and prevents the escape of moisture. One caveat: marinating too long in an active mixture can break down the meat's texture and make it mushy. Two to three hours is long enough for thin, tender cuts of meat or small birds—overnight for roasts, thick steaks, and tougher cuts. The add-in flavor possibilities are endless: herbs and spices, mustard, Worcestershire, onion, garlic, and all kinds of hot sauces, ground chilies, or pastes. A small amount of honey, brown sugar, fruit preserves, or puree can soften a tart marinade. All you need for a pound of meat is $\frac{1}{3}$ to $\frac{1}{2}$ cup. You'd be amazed what your pantry or fridge might offer up to produce a special marinade.

Salsas and Sauces

Whole books have been written about these popular flavor enhancements. Indeed, we've used several throughout this book, although the more subtle the inherent flavor of the grilled food, the more cautious we become. A zesty, complex sauce or salsa can easily upstage a mild fish fillet, veal chop, or spring lamb. Often it's the simple squeeze of lime or dusting of minced fresh herbs that rules success.

Seasoning suggestions: liquid smoke, black pepper, red pepper flakes, hot sauce, garlic, dried herbs or spices, mustard

Timing: overnight for whole chicken or pork loin; 2 to 4 hours for chicken parts or chops

Seafood

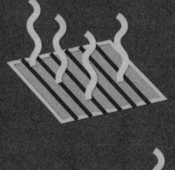

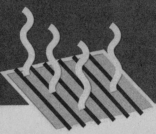

Red Snapper with Black Bean Salsa

Crispy Cajun Catfish with Sun-Dried Tomato Sauce

Grouper Ti-Malice

Cod with Garlic, Capers, and Olives

Halibut with Roasted Garlic and Red Pepper Sauce

Swordfish with Tomato Dill Relish

Maui Mahi-Mahi

Curried Salmon Steak

Salmon Steak with Balsamic Vinegar and Fennel

Danish Mary Bluefish

Tokyo Tuna with Soba Noodles

Tuna Tostadas

Whole Trout Stuffed with Herbs and Toasted Hazelnuts

Skewered Tangerine Scallops

Prosciutto-Wrapped Scallops on Creamy Spinach

Pacific Rim Shrimp

Ginger Shrimp with Mango Mayonnaise

Thai Shrimp Rolls

Linguine with Lobster Tarragon and Charred Yellow Tomatoes

Red Snapper with Black Bean Salsa

We used snapper fillets for this recipe because fillets are what most customers automatically select. If you're cooking outdoors for at least four people, do consider buying the whole gutted fish. The pearly pink beauty of red snapper, ringed with black bean salsa and yellow-green avocado, makes a toast-to-the-host presentation, and the 2½- to 3-pound size of the average fish makes it just right for four. For multiples, the neat little fish will span the grill in regimental form. If you're doing this indoors or just feeling wimpish, use fillets; the flavors will be as complex and tasty. Shallow-fry a basket of quartered corn tortillas to scoop up the salsa.

Serves 4

Salsa:

1 can (15½ ounces) black beans, well rinsed and drained
1 can (14½ ounces) diced tomatoes, drained
¼ cup diced red bell pepper
2 tablespoons minced scallions, white part only
2 tablespoons snipped fresh chives
1 teaspoon grated orange zest
½ teaspoon salt
½ teaspoon freshly ground black pepper
2 teaspoons sherry vinegar
2 teaspoons orange juice
2 tablespoons extra-virgin olive oil
habanero or other hot sauce to taste, optional

1 pound red snapper fillets
canola oil
salt and freshly ground black pepper to taste
sliced avocado dipped in lime juice for garnish

Combine the salsa ingredients and taste for seasoning. Adjust to your preference, if necessary. Set aside. Do not refrigerate unless you are preparing it a day ahead. The salsa should be served at room temperature, not chilled.

Rinse the fillets and pat dry. Coat the fillets with a little oil in the palm of your hand and season lightly with salt and pepper.

Cook the snapper on a stovetop, electric, or outdoor grill for 5 to 6 minutes per side or on a lidded electric grill for a total of 5 to 6 minutes. Serve the fish immediately, surrounded by the salsa and garnished with the avocado slices.

cook's note: If you decide to try a whole snapper on an outdoor grill and you have never done this before, it would be wise to try only one the first time. Use a well-oiled fish basket for easier turning and be certain to have a sturdy large spatula for removing the fish to the serving platter. The only real trick to grilling a whole fish is to keep it intact—losing bits of the skin to the grate or basket is not a disaster.

You needn't be intimidated about serving a whole fish. First, peel off the skin on the face up side. Run a sharp paring knife down the length of the backbone and gently lift the flesh up and away from the skeleton with a fork. It will release easily, leaving the heavier bones behind. After serving half of the fish, simply turn it over and repeat. It's no more difficult than picking clean a whole steamed fish in a Chinese restaurant. Of course, diners should be watchful for small bones that may have broken away from the ribcage.

nutritional breakdown (per serving)

| Calories: 273 | Carbohydrates: 18 g | Protein: 29 g | Fat: 11 g |
| Saturated fat: 1 g | % calories from fat: 35% | Cholesterol: 43 mg | Sodium: 914 mg |

Crispy Cajun Catfish with Sun-Dried Tomato Sauce

Now that catfish is farmed, it has even gained city fans. It's plentiful, inexpensive by fresh fish standards, and has a lovely mild flavor and silky texture. No matter how gentrified it has become, however, it still wants to be fried. We don't pretend this grilled version is equal to a deep-fried fish, but it stands proudly on its own.

Serve these spicy, crunchy fillets with a puree of potato, parsnip, and celery root.

Serves 4

1 pound catfish fillets
plain low-fat yogurt (not nonfat yogurt)
New Orleans fish fry seasoning mix, preferably Zatarain's
cayenne, to taste

Sauce:

4 sun-dried tomatoes in oil
2 garlic cloves, chopped
1 tablespoon fresh lemon juice
salt and freshly ground black pepper to taste
½ cup plain low-fat yogurt
½ cup light mayonnaise, preferably Hellmann's or Best's

inse the fish and pat dry. Spread the fillets lightly but completely with yo-gurt. You need only a thin coating to make the seasoning mix adhere. If you would like to perk up the coating, sprinkle it lightly with cayenne. Press the fillets into the seasoning mix and set them, uncovered, in the refrigerator for at least an hour.

Meanwhile, make the sauce. Mince the tomatoes and garlic in a food processor. Add the lemon juice, salt and pepper, yogurt, and mayonnaise and pulse to com-bine. Scrape into a serving bowl and refrigerate.

Spray the fish lightly with cooking oil spray and cook on a stovetop or electric in-door or outdoor grill for 3½ minutes on each side or 6 minutes altogether on an electric grill with a lid. Serve immediately.

● **nutritional breakdown (per serving)**

Calories: 321	Carbohydrates: 14 g	Protein: 20 g	Fat: 19 g
Saturated fat: 4 g	% calories from fat: 52%	Cholesterol: 72 mg	Sodium: 772 mg

Grouper Ti-Malice

This is an unadulterated hot, tart Haitian classic that begs for a sultry evening, a few friends who want to reminisce about their last memorable trip to the Caribbean, cool rum punches, and a soft calypso beat in the background. Toss some thick slices of parboiled sweet potatoes on the grill and serve a tropical fruit salad.

Serves 4

2 tablespoons canola oil
1 sweet onion, thinly sliced
4 garlic cloves, minced
1 habanero pepper, seeded and minced
salt to taste
½ cup fresh lime juice
1 pound grouper fillets
freshly ground black pepper to taste

Heat the canola oil in a skillet over low heat and sauté the onion slices, covered, until they are soft and beginning to brown. Uncover the skillet, add the garlic and pepper, and continue to sauté until the onion is golden and very soft. Season with salt. Add the lime juice and simmer until the liquid is reduced slightly and the mixture becomes cohesive.

Rinse the fillets and pat dry. Coat them with oily fingers and season lightly with salt and pepper. Cook the grouper on a stovetop, electric, or outdoor grill for 5 to 6 minutes per side. On a lidded electric grill, the fish should be opaque throughout in 5 to 6 minutes with the lid down. Serve the fillets immediately with the onion sauce spooned on top.

nutritional breakdown (per serving)

| Calories: 228 | Carbohydrates: 7 g | Protein: 24 g | Fat: 12 g |
| Saturated fat: 1 g | % calories from fat: 45% | Cholesterol: 43 mg | Sodium: 196 mg |

Cod with Garlic, Capers, and Olives

Sweet, moist codfish takes well to this piquant treatment, but its soft, flaky texture requires careful handling on the grill. Use a fish basket outdoors or on the rotisserie, and if you're going to cook inside, select the thickest fillets and use a wide spatula for turning the fish over.

Serves 4

1 pound cod fillets

2 garlic cloves, smashed and minced

1 teaspoon ground cumin

2 teaspoons canola oil

salt and freshly ground black pepper to taste

2½ tablespoons minced green olives

2½ tablespoons minced capers

1 tablespoon minced parsley

Rinse the fish and pat dry. Combine the garlic, cumin, and oil and rub into the fillets. Lightly season with salt and pepper. Allow the cod to marinate in the oil rub for at least an hour. Combine the olives, capers, and parsley and set aside.

Cook the fish for about 5 minutes on each side on a stovetop, electric, or outdoor grill. In a lidded electric grill, 5 to 6 minutes total should render the fillets opaque throughout.

Serve the cod immediately with the olives, capers, and parsley strewn over the top.

nutritional breakdown (per serving)

Calories: 129	Carbohydrates: 1 g	Protein: 21 g	Fat: 4 g
Saturated fat: 0 g	% calories from fat: 27%	Cholesterol: 51 mg	Sodium: 420 mg

Halibut with Roasted Garlic and Red Pepper Sauce

Our fish purveyor reports that halibut is his fastest-selling fish, and that means cooks are always looking for new ways to serve it. This brilliantly colorful and delicious red pepper sauce utilizes Jacques Pépin's clever method of thickening *aioli* with bread or cooked potato instead of egg yolk. This version uses a lot less oil, and the garlic is roasted rather than raw, as in the Mediterranean mayonnaise. We wanted a more flowing and less intensely flavored sauce for this rather mild fish. Once you've made this sauce, you'll start to find other uses for it. It's a great do-ahead sauce that keeps well in the refrigerator for about a week. It would also complement chicken or lamb, as well provide a handy spread for crostini or focaccia with a heavy grating of Parmesan cheese.

Serves 4

1 garlic head, roasted (see box on next page)
1 slice bread, crusts removed, torn into pieces
1 tablespoon fresh lemon juice
4 bottled or canned whole roasted red peppers (about 1 cup)
¼ teaspoon salt
pinch of cayenne
3 tablespoons extra-virgin olive oil
canned low-sodium chicken broth
1 pound halibut fillets
salt and freshly ground black pepper to taste

Put the garlic pulp in a food processor along with the bread, lemon juice, peppers, salt, and cayenne. Pulse into a thick puree. Slowly add the olive oil in a thin stream as if making mayonnaise. If the sauce needs loosening, process it fur-

To Roast Garlic: Slice off the top of a whole unpeeled head of garlic to expose the tips of the cloves. Place it on a sheet of aluminum foil, sprinkle with salt and pepper, and drizzle with olive oil. Roll up tightly and roast for 1 hour at 350°. Allow it to cool slightly, then squeeze out all the pulp, starting at the bottom of the head and working up to the top.

ther with a little chicken broth. Pour the mixture into a small saucepan and set it on the stove or grill for later warming.

Rinse the fish and pat dry. Season lightly with salt and pepper. Cook on a stove-top, electric, or outdoor grill for 5 to 6 minutes per side or on a lidded electric grill for a total of 5 to 6 minutes. Serve the halibut on top of a puddle of the warm pepper sauce.

cook's note: Small roasted new potatoes would go well with this fish. Par-boil them first and cook them whole on an outdoor grill. Cut them in half to gain stripes on an indoor ridged grill.

● **nutritional breakdown (per serving)**

Calories: 263	Carbohydrates: 9 g	Protein: 26 g	Fat: 14 g
Saturated fat: 2 g	% calories from fat: 46%	Cholesterol: 38 mg	Sodium: 504 mg

Swordfish with Tomato Dill Relish

The dense flesh of swordfish makes it one of the best choices for grilling. The thickness of the steaks and the oily nature of swordfish also make it more foolproof than many of its more delicate cousins, but a watchful eye is still needed to prevent turning it into a Frisbee. The uncooked relish is a bright, perky companion to this sturdy fish and can be put together in a flash. A good alternative to cooking the steak whole is to cut it into cubes and thread onto skewers with parboiled fingerling potato halves and cherry tomatoes. The relish remains complementary, and the meal is nearly complete.

Serves 4

Relish:
1⁄3 cup minced onion
1 tablespoon extra-virgin olive oil
12 cherry tomatoes, squeezed dry and quartered
2 tablespoons minced fresh dill
1½ tablespoon capers, chopped
salt and freshly ground black pepper to taste
olive oil
1 pound swordfish steak, 1 to 1¼ inches thick

Put the onion in a small sieve and slowly pour boiling water through it. Dump the onion into a folded paper towel and blot dry. This will rid the onion of some of its sharp bite. You can omit this step if you have a Vidalia or Maui onion.

Combine the onion with all the remaining relish ingredients and set aside.

Rub or spray a light film of olive oil over the swordfish to prevent sticking. Season with salt and pepper.

Grill the steak on a stovetop, electric, or outdoor grill for 3 to 4 minutes per side or on a lidded electric grill for 5 minutes altogether.

Serve the fish with a pyramid of relish on top.

nutritional breakdown (per serving)

| Calories: 199 | Carbohydrates: 4 g | Protein: 24 g | Fat: 9 g |
| Saturated fat: 2 g | % calories from fat: 42% | Cholesterol: 46 mg | Sodium: 425 mg |

Maui Mahi-Mahi

Grilled tropical fruit was one of the sideline revelations of the new American cuisine, and creative restaurant chefs soon introduced us to grilling it with fish. It takes some discretion to combine fruit with fish, and this recipe, with its decided South Pacific twist, is a good primer. The zippy pineapple sauce could also be served with poultry or pork.

Serves 4

1 pound mahi-mahi fillets
salt and freshly ground black pepper to taste
Asian sesame seed oil

Sauce:

3 or 4 thick slices fresh pineapple
6 scallions, white part chopped with 1 inch of the green
3 quarter-size coins fresh ginger, peeled and minced
1 tablespoon minced hot red pepper
pinch of salt
¼ cup white wine, dry sherry, or low-sodium chicken broth
1 tablespoon minced fresh cilantro
2 teaspoons toasted sesame seeds, optional

Rinse the fillets and pat them dry. Season with salt and pepper and, with fingers dipped in the oil, very lightly coat the fish. Set aside.

Place the pineapple slices on a hot grill and sear them until caramelized stripes appear. Roughly chop enough of the pineapple to fill a 1-cup measure. Set aside.

In a small microwave-safe bowl, cover the scallions, ginger, hot peppers, and salt with the wine and cook on high for 1 minute. Combine with the grilled pineapple, cilantro, and sesame seeds.

Cook the fish on a stovetop, electric, or outdoor grill for 3 minutes per side or on a lidded electric grill for 4 to 5 minutes total.

Serve the mahi-mahi with the grilled pineapple relish to one side.

● **nutritional breakdown (per serving)**

Calories: 156	Carbohydrates: 6 g	Protein: 22 g	Fat: 3 g
Saturated fat: 1 g	% calories from fat: 19%	Cholesterol: 87 mg	Sodium: 299 mg

Curried Salmon Steak

If salmon isn't your favorite fish but you keep trying because of its well-proclaimed health benefits, this recipe might make you a convert. You can keep the 1-2-3 sauce warm right on the edge of the stovetop or grill. This hot-sweet sauce can be addictive, so we're pleased to report that you can also enjoy it over grilled chicken, lamb, shrimp, or scallops.

Serves 4

4 salmon steaks, 1 inch thick
canola oil
salt and freshly ground black pepper to taste

Sauce:
1 cup unsweetened coconut milk
1 teaspoon Thai red curry paste
1 tablespoon light brown sugar
1½ tablespoons fresh lime juice
pinch of salt
2 teaspoons cornstarch
8 fresh basil leaves

Rub the salmon steaks with a light coating of oil. Season with salt and pepper. Cook them on a hot stovetop, electric, or outside grill for about 10 minutes or on a lidded electric grill for 5 to 6 minutes.

Meanwhile, heat all the sauce ingredients except the cornstarch and basil in a small saucepan. Taste and adjust the seasoning to your preference. Mix the cornstarch with a small amount of water to make a slurry. Just before the salmon is done, add it to the sauce and stir until it is glossy and coats the back of a spoon. Stack and roll up the basil leaves like a small cigar. Sliver them crosswise into narrow ribbons and drop into the sauce. Keep the sauce warm, but don't simmer it longer or its magic powers will diminish.

Serve the salmon immediately with the sauce over it.

cook's note: This is a wonderful company dish for those times when you can barely beat your guests to the door. To present it in the special manner they no doubt deserve, search out Forbidden Rice—a black variety from China. It looks like shiny caviar on the plate and has an elusive, musky quality and an appealing chewiness. A few chive pick-up sticks over it all will make you proud.

nutritional breakdown (per serving)

Calories: 441	Carbohydrates: 9 g	Protein: 30 g	Fat: 32 g
Saturated fat: 16 g	% calories from fat: 65%	Cholesterol: 80 mg	Sodium: 302 mg

Salmon Steak with Balsamic Vinegar and Fennel

Balsamic vinegar gives grilled salmon a lovely sweet-sour glaze, and crushed fennel seeds add a subtle touch of anise. Altogether, this is a lovely, unusual, and elegant way to serve the ubiquitous salmon and a great way to use the underappreciated vegetable fennel.

Serves 4

4 salmon steaks
2 tablespoons fennel seeds
salt and freshly ground black pepper to taste
⅓ cup balsamic vinegar
4 small fennel bulbs
canola oil
¼ cup grated carrot

Rinse the salmon and pat dry. Crush the fennel seeds in a spice mill or in a heavy plastic bag with a rolling pin. Rub the crushed seeds into the salmon and lightly season with salt and pepper. Lay the steaks side by side in a shallow dish. Pour the balsamic vinegar over the top and set aside for at least 1 hour.

Remove the stalk and root end of the fennel, discarding the tough outer layer. Cut the bulbs in half and put them in a covered microwave-safe dish with a little water or canned chicken broth. Season with salt and pepper. Cook on high for 3 to 4 minutes, or until just tender when pierced with the tip of a sharp paring knife. Drain and pat dry. Coat the fennel lightly with oily fingers.

Lift the salmon from the marinade, letting the excess drip back into the dish. Pour the marinade into a small microwave-safe dish and bring it to a boil. Set aside.

Cook the salmon and fennel on a stovetop, electric, or outdoor grill for about 6 minutes per side or on a lidded electric grill for 7 to 8 minutes with the lid down. The fish should be opaque all the way through and the fennel nicely striped with golden brown.

Serve the salmon with the marinade drizzled over the top, and the fennel sprinkled with the grated carrot.

● **nutritional breakdown (per serving)**

Calories: 364	Carbohydrates: 18 g	Protein: 31 g	Fat: 19 g
Saturated fat: 3 g	% calories from fat: 46%	Cholesterol: 80 mg	Sodium: 465 mg

Danish Mary Bluefish

Grilled bluefish and a Danish Mary sounded like a swell idea, so we put them together for an interesting taste treat. Oskar Davidson's in Copenhagen might do well to add this to their smorrebröd menu. Bluefish is assertive enough to stand up to this treatment, as is mackerel. Small red potatoes with butter and dill would be the best accompaniment.

Serves 4

Marinade:

1¼ cups tomato juice

¼ cup aquavit (Danish liquor)

1 teaspoon sugar

1 teaspoon celery salt

½ teaspoon caraway seeds

1 tablespoon fresh lemon juice

1½ teaspoons Worcestershire sauce

½ teaspoon Tabasco, or to taste

1 pound bluefish fillets

flour

2 teaspoons arrowroot

⅓ cup canned diced tomato

Put all the ingredients for the marinade in a glass 2-cup measure and microwave on high for 3 minutes. Cool.

Pour the marinade over the fish in a covered dish and marinate for 1 to 2 hours. Drain, reserving the marinade in a small saucepan. Spoon a little flour into a small sieve and lightly dust the fillets. Add the arrowroot to the marinade and simmer until velvety and thick enough to coat the back of a spoon. Add the diced tomato and keep the sauce warm.

Grill the fish indoors or out. It will take about 3 minutes per side on an open electric, stovetop, or outside grill and 4 minutes total on an electric grill with a lid. Serve immediately, napped with the sauce.

nutritional breakdown (per serving)

Calories: 198	Carbohydrates: 10 g	Protein: 25 g	Fat: 5 g
Saturated fat: 1 g	% calories from fat: 23%	Cholesterol: 70 mg	Sodium: 826 mg

Tokyo Tuna with Soba Noodles

Someone reported recently that the price for the very best tuna in Japan could top $20,000, dead in the water. Of course, that's for a giant fish so fresh and pristine it's expected to be savored raw. We have the Japanese to thank for teaching us the difference between assertive canned tuna and a fresh steak of such tenderness and delicacy it can tolerate mere minutes on the grill—and there's the rub. The highly nutritious omega oil throughout its fine texture conducts the heat as rapidly as it drains out, and therefore, if tuna is cooked throughout, it will turn as dry and flavorless as cotton batting. If you've tried cooking tuna and that's what happened, try again.

Serves 4

Glaze:

¼ cup Japanese soy sauce

½ cup sake

3 tablespoons mirin (sweet rice wine)

2 teaspoons sugar

2 small dried red chilies, seeded and chopped

3 quarter-size coins fresh ginger, peeled and slivered

12 ounces fresh yellowfin tuna, 1 inch thick

coarse salt

½ pound soba (buckwheat noodles) or angel hair pasta, cooked

1 cup shredded or grated daikon for garnish

¼ cup snipped fresh chives for garnish

Combine the glaze ingredients in a glass 2-cup measure and microwave on high for 3 minutes. Set aside to cool. Strain.

Sprinkle the tuna with coarse salt and dip it in a little of the glaze just before grilling. Quickly sear the fish on both sides on a stovetop or electric grill or on an outdoor barbecue. This will take a minute on each side. Brush it generously with the glaze and cook it for another minute on each side. Check for doneness at 30-second intervals, brushing with the glaze at each turn, keeping in mind that it will cook further between the heat and the plate. The inside should be grayish pink with a translucent red stripe in the center.

Reheat the noodles. If you're cooking outdoors, this can be done in a skillet on top of the grill. Indoors, they can be reheated briefly in the microwave or in a skillet on the stovetop. Slice the tuna about ¼ inch thick and arrange the slices over individual servings of noodles. Drizzle the remaining glaze over the tuna. Sprinkle the daikon and chives on top and pass out the chopsticks.

nutritional breakdown (per serving)

Calories: 166	Carbohydrates: 10 g	Protein: 23 g	Fat: 1 g
Saturated fat: 0 g	% calories from fat: 4%	Cholesterol: 41 mg	Sodium: 1,110 mg

Tuna Tostadas

This spin on the Baja fish taco sounds too simple to taste so special. It may also sound too rich to dare, but one of these *grande* tostadas is a substantial meal and well worth the occasional indulgence. The recipe deserves the very brightest, most translucent red tuna you can find. While you're at it, there are now traditional New Mexico flour tortillas being distributed to specialty supermarkets. There is little comparison between these thin, ethereal treats and the tire patches we've gnawed through in the past. Look for them.

Serves 4

3 tablespoons canola oil
4 8-inch flour tortillas
1 ripe avocado
juice of ½ lime
salt to taste
¼ cup minced fresh cilantro
8 romaine leaves
1 large ripe tomato, halved, pulped, and seeded
6 tablespoons light sour cream
1 teaspoon pureed chipotle en adobo
12 ounces fresh tuna loin, cut ¾ inch thick

Heat the oil over medium-high heat in a medium skillet. Crisp each tortilla on both sides until light golden brown and drain on paper towels. Set one on each serving plate to cool.

Mash the avocado, lime juice, salt, and cilantro with a fork until smooth. Spread an equal quantity on each tostada. Break off the thickest white stem of the romaine. Stack and roll 3 or 4 leaves at a time and cut across the roll into fine ribbons. Distribute them over the avocado. Sliver the tomato shell and arrange on top of the lettuce. Lightly salt the surface.

Combine the sour cream and chipotle pepper puree. Set aside.

Coat the surface of the tuna with lightly oiled fingers. Cook it in a lidded electric grill for about 3 minutes or until the center shows a ¼-inch-wide streak of red. Do not allow the tuna to cook all the way through or it will be dry and tasteless. If using an outdoor grill, cook the tuna about 2 minutes per side.

Cut the tuna in thin strips and arrange them like spokes around the tostada. Put a generous dollop of the spicy sour cream mixture in the center.

cook's note: This recipe can also be made successfully with grilled grouper or red snapper.

The tortillas can be crisped in a 375° oven, directly on the middle rack, for about 5 minutes, or until flaky and crisp.

nutritional breakdown (per serving)

Calories: 446	Carbohydrates: 39 g	Protein: 29 g	Fat: 19 g
Saturated fat: 4 g	% calories from fat: 39%	Cholesterol: 49 mg	Sodium: 503 mg

Whole Trout Stuffed with Herbs and Toasted Hazelnuts

How often have you passed up a glistening whole rainbow trout in favor of fillets just because the eyes stared back? Buying a gutted trout for the grill is the only way to go, because fillets are far too delicate to withstand intense heat and the skin provides natural protection. The neat little fish is hinged at the backbone, which makes infusing the flesh with aromatics simple: all you need to do is open it like a book and tuck the seasoning inside. There is no more striking centerpiece for an outdoor buffet than perfectly grilled trout placed nose to nose around a platter lined with shredded leaf lettuce. Summer ripe tomatoes from a local farm stand and steamed new potatoes with lemon vinaigrette could complete the feast.

Serves 4

⅓ cup whole hazelnuts
4 gutted whole rainbow trout, 6 to 7 ounces each
1 tablespoon soft unsalted butter
2 garlic cloves, smashed and minced
salt and freshly ground black pepper to taste
4 full sprigs fresh tarragon
6 full stems flat-leaf parsley
4 teaspoons snipped fresh chives
canola oil

Toast the hazelnuts in a 300° oven for about 6 minutes, or until you can smell their fragrance. When they are cool enough to handle, remove the skins by rubbing them vigorously in a paper towel. Don't fret if you can't remove all of the skins. Chop the nuts and set aside.

Rinse the trout and pat dry. Open each one and spread with butter and sprinkle with garlic. Season with salt and pepper. Pull the leaves from the tarragon and parsley and distribute over both sides of the open fish, along with the chives and hazelnuts. Close the trout and lightly coat the skin with canola oil.

Total cooking time on a stovetop, electric, or outdoor grill will be about 6 minutes per side. In a lidded electric grill, a total of 6 minutes should produce a crispy skin and moist flesh.

nutritional breakdown (per serving)

Calories: 370	Carbohydrates: 3 g	Protein: 36 g	Fat: 23 g
Saturated fat: 6 g	% calories from fat: 57%	Cholesterol: 105 mg	Sodium: 237 mg

Grilling Shellfish

All shellfish is sublime cooked outdoors over charcoal. The shells of lobsters, crabs, shrimp, oysters, mussels, and clams protect the tender flesh from the direct heat, and the smoke imparts a subtle and memorable flavor. Here are a few tips for success:

- Lobsters should be split and eviscerated, which your seafood purveyor can do. Have this done as close to cooking time as possible; once killed, lobsters should be cooked immediately. If you have the stomach to do the job yourself, make a quick and merciful knife thrust just behind the eyes. Then grill the lobsters immediately, split or whole.

- Bivalves need no preparation other than scrubbing. Farmed mussels need no debearding, but if you're lucky enough to find wild ones, yank off any strands poking out of their shells. Discard any mussel, oyster, or clam shells that have opened before cooking unless they close again when lightly tapped.

- Jumbo shrimp are the best choice for the grill, and skewering them makes turning them over easier. Or you can use a hinged basket to contain them.

- Build a medium-hot fire, allowing the coals to develop a coat of white ash. Always oil the grate as well as the shells of the fish.

- Place the shellfish 4 to 5 inches above the coals.

- Crustaceans should be basted with oil during cooking to keep them moist. The oil can be plain or flavored. Split lobster calls for melted butter to be drizzled over the flesh, and excellent choices for seasoning it are fresh tarragon, chives, or lemon.

- Have any sauces, dips, or condiments ready before you start. Cooking time is brief, so the guests must wait—not the fish.

- Crustaceans are ready when the flesh is firm and opaque. Bivalves are ready as soon as the shells have opened.

Approximate cooking times are:

Lobster, 12–15 minutes

Dungeness crabs, 10–12 minutes

Soft-shell crabs, oysters, and clams, 8–10 minutes

Shrimp, 4–5 minutes

Skewered Tangerine Scallops

The meaty, muscular sea scallop is ideal for threading on skewers since it was so cleverly designed for portion control. Scallops are one of the most succulent creatures of the sea and need little embellishment to make a superb meal. Although they have no fat, they seem rich on the palate, and four large scallops are quite enough for one person. Considering their expense, this is a good thing. Be sure to select the pale ivory, sticky ones, and don't be fooled into buying the pristine white ones floating around in cloudy liquid. They've been chemically injected for a longer shelf life and will exude water annoyingly when you try to cook them. Also, be certain to pull off the small white connector tab on the side of the scallop—it can be very bitter.

Serves 4

16 large sea scallops
⅓ cup bottled yakitori sauce
¼ cup tangerine or orange juice
½ teaspoon grated tangerine or orange zest
juice of ½ lime
pinch of sugar
2 teaspoons hot Asian chili sauce
2 teaspoons cornstarch
fragrant peanut or canola oil
1 tablespoon snipped fresh chives for garnish

Put the scallops in a medium bowl and add the yakitori sauce, tangerine juice and zest, lime juice, sugar, and chili sauce. Stir to combine. Marinate for at least 1 hour. Remove the scallops with a slotted spoon, preserving the marinade, and skewer them for grilling. Put the cornstarch in a tiny dish and drizzle in a couple of tablespoons of the marinade to make a slurry for thickening. Set it aside.

Brush the scallops with oil and cook them for 4 minutes on a stovetop, electric, or outdoor grill. Check for doneness after 3 minutes on a lidded electric grill. It's a matter of preference whether scallops are cooked all the way through or still display a translucent center. They are not harmful if eaten raw or underdone.

While the scallops are grilling, heat the marinade to a simmer either in the microwave or on the stove. Add the cornstarch slurry and cook until the sauce is lightly thickened and glossy. Spoon the sauce over the scallops and garnish with the snipped chives.

● **nutritional breakdown (per serving)**

Calories: 183	Carbohydrates: 18 g	Protein: 15 g	Fat: 5 g
Saturated fat: 0 g	% calories from fat: 26%	Cholesterol: 27 mg	Sodium: 1,000 mg

Prosciutto-Wrapped Scallops on Creamy Spinach

We can't take credit for this combination—it was inspired. At first glance the cream might give you pause, but there's little other fat in this meal, so the minimal amount per person isn't such a wild transgression.

Serves 4

6 paper-thin slices imported prosciutto
16 large sea scallops
2 bags of fresh baby spinach, about 1½ pounds
½ cup heavy cream
salt and freshly ground black pepper to taste
freshly grated nutmeg to taste
4 lemon wedges

Tear or slice the ham into long, thin strips and wrap a strip around the sides of each scallop, fastening it with a toothpick. There's no need for neat edges, nor do the strips need to be of equal length. Set the scallops aside for grilling.

Sprinkle or spray the spinach with a little water and blanch it in a large covered skillet or wok until it wilts. You may have to do this in relays, but each round will take only a few seconds. Dump the spinach into a colander and press out as much water as possible. Place the spinach on a cutting board and chop it roughly.

Heat the cream in a medium saucepan and add the spinach. Lift and toss it with tongs to combine thoroughly. Season with salt and pepper and a touch of grated nutmeg. Slide the pan off the heat.

Grill the scallops for 4 minutes on a stovetop, electric, or outdoor grill. Check for doneness after 3 minutes on a lidded electric grill. It's a matter of preference whether scallops are cooked all the way through or still display a translucent center. They are not harmful if eaten raw or underdone.

While the scallops are grilling, return the spinach to the heat and bring to a simmer. Cook until the cream thickens. Should the mixture become too dry, add a little milk to moisten.

Pull the toothpicks from the scallops and serve the scallops on top of a serving of the creamed spinach with a lemon wedge to the side.

cook's note: If you want to gild the lily, a few toasted pine nuts would be a tasty garnish for this dish.

● **nutritional breakdown (per serving)**

Calories: 237	Carbohydrates: 3 g	Protein: 23 g	Fat: 15 g
Saturated fat: 7 g	% calories from fat: 58%	Cholesterol: 78 mg	Sodium: 1,078 mg

Pacific Rim Shrimp

This is the next best thing to deep-fried coconut shrimp, so when you have a hankering, pick up some jumbo shrimp and fire up the grill. The sauce is good enough to eat with a spoon, so be sure to serve generous bowls of rice to soak it up. Ice-cold beer will put out the fire.

Serves 4

½ cup unsweetened coconut milk
2 tablespoons fresh lime juice
¼ cup soy sauce
1 teaspoon grated fresh ginger, with the juice
1 tablespoon sugar
2 teaspoons hot Asian chili paste, preferably with garlic
1 pound jumbo shrimp, shelled and deveined, tails on
3 tablespoons unsweetened flake coconut, toasted, for garnish
minced fresh cilantro for garnish

In a bowl large enough to hold the shrimp, combine the coconut milk, lime juice, soy sauce, ginger, sugar, and chili paste. Add the shrimp and marinate for 30 minutes. Pour the marinade into a small saucepan and simmer until slightly thickened. Do not boil. Keep the sauce warm.

Cook the shrimp for 2 to 3 minutes on a stovetop, electric, or outdoor grill. The shrimp are done when they are just a bit springy to the pressure of your finger. Serve immediately with the sauce drizzled over them and the toasted coconut and cilantro on top.

nutritional breakdown (per serving)

Calories: 207	Carbohydrates: 8 g	Protein: 23 g	Fat: 10 g
Saturated fat: 8 g	% calories from fat: 41%	Cholesterol: 193 mg	Sodium: 1,242 mg

Ginger Shrimp with Mango Mayonnaise

Almost nothing holds more appeal than grilled shrimp, and except for a few minutes of peeling and deveining, they couldn't be easier or more foolproof to prepare. One needs only to avoid the danger of overcooking, which can happen just in the time that it takes to remove all the shrimp from the heat. The best way to solve this is to use a grill basket or thread the shrimp onto skewers. Cooking them in their shells helps a lot too, but your family or guests may not be happy having to work for their supper.

Good shrimp need little embellishment. The ginger-garlic oil adds just the right tang to their natural ocean flavor, and the spicy mango dip is an embellishment that, incidentally, would be equally complementary to grilled sea scallops, salmon kabobs, or chilled cocktail shrimp.

Serves 4

1 pound jumbo shrimp, shelled and deveined, tails on
2 tablespoons canola oil
3 garlic cloves, smashed and minced
2 teaspoons grated fresh ginger, with the juice
1 ripe mango
¼ cup light mayonnaise, preferably Hellmann's or Best's
1½ teaspoons Dijon mustard
1 teaspoon hot sauce, or to taste
pinch of salt

Place the shrimp in a plastic bag. Combine the oil, garlic, and ginger and pour over the shrimp. Twist the bag shut and squish the oil through the shrimp to coat. Refrigerate for 2 to 3 hours or overnight.

Place the mango on its plump round bottom and slice down along either side of the center pit. Make several diagonal slashes through the flesh but not through the skin. Press up on the skin while pressing down on the sides and the mango will turn inside out, exposing the flesh. Cut or scoop it out into a food processor and puree. Add the mayonnaise, mustard, hot sauce, and salt. Continue to puree until the mixture is smooth. Refrigerate.

Cook the shrimp on a stovetop grill for about 2½ minutes per side or on a lidded electric grill for 3 to 4 minutes with the lid down. Over white-ash coals on an outdoor grill, they should be springy to the touch in about 5 minutes. Serve immediately with the mango mayonnaise on the side.

nutritional breakdown (per serving)

Calories: 242	Carbohydrates: 11 g	Protein: 20 g	Fat: 13 g
Saturated fat: 2 g	% calories from fat: 48%	Cholesterol: 185 mg	Sodium: 376 mg

Thai Shrimp Rolls

Here's a fancy way to use small shrimp not macho enough for the barbie. These little bundles, pretty as a Thai dancer, look exotic and exude those palate-tickling Asian flavors we've grown to love. Rather than risk toughening the shrimp, we rolled them in lettuce leaves for protection. To our delight, it worked. The bright green wrapper looked like Christmas paper and was as appetizing as it was practical. If you seal the rolls separately in plastic wrap and store them in a freezer bag, you'll be ready to grill them for family or spur-of-the-moment guests. You could also make the rolls walnut size and steam them for canapés, or mound them on a buffet platter.

Serves 4

6 scallions, white plus 1 inch of the green
3 garlic cloves, peeled and smashed
2 quarter-size coins fresh ginger, peeled and chopped
1 fresh hot red or green pepper, seeded
3 tablespoons fresh cilantro and/or mint leaves
2 tablespoons grated carrot
1 egg white
1 pound medium or small shrimp, shelled and deveined
1 tablespoon cornstarch
1 tablespoon fresh lime juice
1 teaspoon Asian fish sauce (*nam pla*), optional
4 large romaine lettuce leaves

Mince the scallions, garlic, ginger, hot pepper, and cilantro in a food processor. Scrape the mixture out into a bowl and add the grated carrot. Whip the egg white in the processor until foamy and add the shrimp. Pulse until the shrimp are finely chopped but not a paste. Turn out into the bowl and combine with the scallion mixture.

Stir the cornstarch into the combined lime juice and fish sauce. Stir into the shrimp mixture.

Wet your fingers and divide the mixture into 8 balls. Pat them into fat, even sausage shapes. Cut out the thick white stem of the romaine and slice each leaf in half lengthwise. Spray a cutting board lightly with cooking oil and lay out 8 leaf wrappers. Tightly roll up the shrimp sausages in the wrappers and stack them, flap side down. The oil will hold the flaps down and protect the lettuce from burning.

Cook the rolls on a stovetop or electric grill (lid up) for 3 to 4 minutes per side or until firm. On a banked white-ash fire, they should take about 6 minutes altogether.

cook's note: If you're cooking outdoors, run water-soaked wooden skewers lengthwise through each roll to make them easier to turn. Even if you grill them indoors, pierce them with skewers to serve—they look more fetching and authentic.

● **nutritional breakdown (per serving)**

Calories: 136	Carbohydrates: 6 g	Protein: 20 g	Fat: 3 g
Saturated fat: 0 g	% calories from fat: 18%	Cholesterol: 140 mg	Sodium: 157 mg

Linguine with Lobster Tarragon and Charred Yellow Tomatoes

It would be hard to imagine a more elegant dinner that requires so little time and attention. This dish is a good reason to keep lobster tails in the freezer. The other ingredients are generally in the good cook's pantry, so one needs only to pick up fresh tomatoes and tarragon to provide family or friends with a serious treat.

Serves 4

¾ pound imported linguine

2 tablespoons extra-virgin olive oil

2 tablespoons unsalted butter

2 shallots, minced

3 garlic cloves, smashed and minced

salt and generous amounts of freshly ground black pepper

1 tablespoon sun-dried tomato paste (available in tubes or jars)

2½ tablespoons minced fresh tarragon

2 lobster tails, 6 to 8 ounces each

2 large, firm yellow tomatoes, stemmed and halved

Cook the pasta in a stockpot filled with rapidly boiling well-salted water for 8 to 10 minutes, or until al dente. Drain and cool slightly. Coat your hands with a little olive oil and run them through the pasta to keep it from sticking. Set aside.

Heat the olive oil and butter in a large skillet. Add the shallots, garlic, and salt and pepper. Sauté 2 to 3 minutes, or until the shallots soften. Stir in the tomato paste and tarragon and combine.

Slide the sharp point of kitchen shears under one corner of the soft shell on the underside of each lobster tail, above the flesh. Cut all the way around and pull the soft shell off in one piece. Cut lengthwise down the center of the flesh and crack the outer shell just a bit by pushing down on each side with your thumbs. This will flatten the tail slightly. Moisten the meat of each tail with a couple of teaspoons of the tarragon mixture.

Cook the lobster tails, shell down, in a lidded electric grill for about 4 minutes, or until the meat is opaque and firm. On an outdoor grill over white-ash coals, they should take 5 to 6 minutes with the lid down. Remove from the heat and cover lightly with aluminum foil to keep warm.

Char the tomato halves, skin side down, in a lidded electric grill or over charcoal for 3 to 4 minutes, or until just softened and the skins have black stripes. Let them cool a little, pull off the skins, and chop coarsely. Add to the remaining tarragon mixture in the skillet and toss with the cooked linguine. Reheat in the skillet.

Pull the meat from the lobster tails and cut it into chunks. Divide the pasta among 4 heated flat-rimmed bowls and arrange the lobster on top. Serve immediately.

No cheese on this dish, please.

nutritional breakdown (per serving)

Calories: 541	Carbohydrates: 72 g	Protein: 25 g	Fat: 17 g
Saturated fat: 5 g	% calories from fat: 27%	Cholesterol: 62 mg	Sodium: 503 mg

Burgers and Pizza

Green Chili Burger

Carib Beef and Mango Burger

Hamburger Siciliano

Bacon and Cheese Chicken Burger

Orange Salmon Burger

Open-Face Catfish Burger

Red, White, and Blue Buffalo Burger

Apple and Shiitake Venison Burger

Mushroom, Barley, and Hazelnut Burger

Grilled Pizza

   Roasted Eggplant and Peppers

   Charred Red and White Onions with Prosciutto and Black Walnuts

   Roasted Garlic, Baby Spinach, and Grape Tomatoes

   White Pizza Portobello

Green Chili Burger

This unusual and superb hamburger is a local favorite in Santa Fe restaurants, where welcoming dried chili peppers are hung on *casita* doors and even find their way into peanut brittle (although the latter is undoubtedly for the amusement of tourists). Santa Fe peppers are sublime but rarely make it beyond local and West Coast markets, so we've substituted a selection of both mild and hot green chili peppers increasingly available in supermarkets and specialty food stores. Unless you're particularly fond of them, the only no-no is the green bell pepper, which lends too grassy a taste to the mix. Poblanos and pasillas are worth the search, and the small zippy jalapeño is a must. The flesh of the serrano is so thin it will disintegrate over live coals, but it cooks quickly enough on a stovetop or electric grill for you to lift the papery skin before it blackens. The selection and the roasting of the peppers are what make this burger, so gather them when you can. They can be roasted ahead, drizzled lightly with oil, and kept in the refrigerator for about a week.

Serves 4

2 poblano peppers
2 pasilla peppers
3 Anaheim peppers
3 jalapeño peppers, or 2 jalapeños and 1 serrano
drizzle of olive or canola oil
salt and freshly ground black pepper to taste
1 pound ground chuck or sirloin
4 hamburger buns

The peppers are best roasted over a hot charcoal grill, but they can be charred on a stovetop or lidded grill or under a hot broiler. The goal is to blacken the skin all over without softening the flesh so much that it causes the peppers to collapse. Once they are charred, drop the peppers into a plastic bag and let them steam for at least 10 minutes. When they're cool enough to handle, rub the skins from the flesh with your fingers. Do this over the sink with the water running so you can keep rinsing your fingers (not the peppers, or you'll lose the flavorful oils). Ignore small flecks of black skin that don't pick off easily—they announce the peppers are roasted.

Cut around the base of the stem with a sharp paring knife and pull out the stem along with the seedpod. Pull the peppers apart along the rib lines. If the sections are too large, tear them in half. Flick off any seeds adhering to the inside of the flesh and put the strips (called *rajas*) in a bowl with a light drizzle of olive or canola oil. Season lightly with salt and black pepper.

Form the beef into 4 patties and cook on an indoor lidded grill for 3 to 5 minutes or over white-ash charcoal outdoors about 3 minutes per side.

Grill the buns, place the burgers on the bottom half, and crisscross a lavish heap of *rajas* on top. *Muy, muy bueno!*

● **nutritional breakdown (per serving)**

Calories: 319	Carbohydrates: 12 g	Protein: 24 g	Fat: 20 g
Saturated fat: 7 g	% calories from fat: 56%	Cholesterol: 74 mg	Sodium: 221 mg

● **(with bun)**

Calories: 442	Carbohydrates: 34 g	Protein: 27 g	Fat: 22 g
Saturated fat: 7 g	% calories from fat: 45%	Cholesterol: 74 mg	Sodium: 462 mg

Carib Beef and Mango Burger

If there isn't a sassy, spicy hamburger like this anywhere in the Caribbean, there ought to be. Maybe some island will adopt it and give it one of those rhythmic calypso names, like Stamp and Man-go. The tropical appeal of this burger makes it ideal for the outdoor grill, tall frosty drinks, and big bowls of plantain chips. But if you can't wait for warm weather, they're sure to turn a cold winter night hot.

Serves 4 or 5

1 pound ground chuck or sirloin
½ cup minced onion
1 teaspoon freshly grated nutmeg
½ teaspoon salt
freshly ground black pepper to taste
2 to 3 tablespoons Caribbean hot sauce
1 ripe mango
½ lime
4 or 5 hamburger buns, split and buttered
red leaf lettuce

Put the ground beef on a clean cutting board and combine it with the onion, nutmeg, salt, pepper, and hot sauce by gently pulling the clumps of meat apart and working the seasonings into the meat with your fingers. Keep the mixture as loose as possible, or you'll end up with leaden patties. Divide the meat into 4 giant servings or 5 more modest ones.

Slice the mango by standing it on its plump bottom and cutting down on either side as close to the pit as possible. Peel each side with a sharp paring knife and slice thinly lengthwise. Set aside on a plate and squeeze lime juice over the slices.

The burgers will take only 3 to 4 minutes to cook on an indoor lidded grill and about 5 minutes on a stovetop or outdoor grill over white-ash coals.

Toast the buns. Line the bottoms with a lettuce leaf and a slice of mango and place a burger on top. Serve with packaged plantain chips.

cook's treat: Peel off the skin from the edges remaining on the pit. Standing over the sink, pull off the juicy flesh clinging to the pit with your teeth. It's the best.

nutritional breakdown (per serving)

Calories: 279	Carbohydrates: 12 g	Protein: 22 g	Fat: 16 g
Saturated fat: 6 g	% calories from fat: 51%	Cholesterol: 74 mg	Sodium: 947 mg

(with bun)

Calories: 429	Carbohydrates: 33 g	Protein: 25 g	Fat: 21 g
Saturated fat: 9 g	% calories from fat: 44%	Cholesterol: 82 mg	Sodium: 1,219 mg

Hamburger Siciliano

Italians like hamburgers too, and this one is redolent of the essence of Sicily. Olives, capers, and anchovies find their way into many Sicilian dishes. The interior surprise of these zesty, sunny island flavors would have made Garibaldi sing. Serve these burgers on a crusty, partially hollowed-out roll with a slice of summer ripe tomato.

Serves 4

1½ tablespoons chopped Sicilian green olives
1½ tablespoons minced onion
1½ tablespoons chopped capers
4 flat anchovy fillets, minced
1 pound ground chuck
olive oil
salt and freshly ground black pepper to taste

Combine the olives, onion, capers, and anchovies. Form the meat into 4 fat balls. With the tip of a dinner knife, push a wide pocket into the meat and insert an equal share of the filling into each ball. Press the pocket closed and flatten the meat gently. Drizzle a little oil into the palm of your hands and coat the hamburgers lightly. Season with salt and pepper.

Cook on a stovetop, electric, or outdoor grill for about 3 minutes per side or on an indoor lidded grill for 4 to 5 minutes total.

- **nutritional breakdown (per serving)**

  | Calories: 260 | Carbohydrates: 0 g | Protein: 22 g | Fat: 18 g |
  | Saturated fat: 7 g | % calories from fat: 63% | Cholesterol: 77 mg | Sodium: 447 mg |

- **(with bun)**

  | Calories: 427 | Carbohydrates: 31 g | Protein: 28 g | Fat: 21 g |
  | Saturated fat: 7 g | % calories from fat: 43% | Cholesterol: 77 mg | Sodium: 757 mg |

Bacon and Cheese Chicken Burger

Chicken, cheese, and bacon aren't a novel combination, but these burgers prove they're still one of the best. Charcoal grilling adds another subtle flavor note. Indoor grilling sears the surface quickly, keeping the burgers from becoming dry, as does the use of a little moistening sour cream. They stand alone very well and could be served bunless with, for instance, a spoonful of the lemony Tomato Marmalade on page 86. They would also be successful made with ground turkey.

Serves 4 or 5

6 thin slices smoky bacon
4 thin slices sweet onion, minced
salt and freshly ground black pepper to taste
cayenne to taste
¼ cup minced fresh basil
1½ tablespoons light sour cream
⅓ cup grated Monterey Jack or Gruyère cheese
1 pound ground chicken or turkey
cornmeal
4 or 5 hamburger buns, grilled
leaf lettuce
avocado and tomato slices

Fry the bacon until crisp. Remove from the skillet to drain and cool on paper towels. Crumble into small bits and reserve.

Drain off most of the bacon fat from the skillet, leaving a thin film. Add the onion and cook until softened. Add the seasonings, basil, and sour cream and stir to combine. Cool.

Sprinkle the reserved bacon bits and cheese onto a cutting board, place the meat on the board, and separate it as well as you can with your fingers. Ground chicken is very sticky and more easily worked with moist hands. Turn out the seasoned onion mixture on top and combine all the ingredients by fluffing and folding the meat several times without compacting it. Shape it into 4 large balls or 5 smaller ones. Roll them lightly in cornmeal and press gently into patties.

On a stovetop or outdoor grill over white-ash coals, cook the burgers about 5 minutes. On an indoor grill with a lid, 3 to 4 minutes total. Test to be certain the center is opaque.

Serve on grilled buns lined with lettuce, avocado, and tomato.

nutritional breakdown (per serving)

Calories: 300	Carbohydrates: 5 g	Protein: 24 g	Fat: 20 g
Saturated fat: 4 g	% calories from fat: 58%	Cholesterol: 19 mg	Sodium: 409 mg

(with bun)

Calories: 423	Carbohydrates: 26 g	Protein: 28 g	Fat: 22 g
Saturated fat: 5 g	% calories from fat: 46%	Cholesterol: 19 mg	Sodium: 649 mg

Orange Salmon Burger

Salmon is the leading fish fillet sold today, which means that we've smartly recognized its healthful properties but that we're probably straining for new ways to prepare it. This burger is a fresh and toothsome offering even salmon phobics will applaud. Once again, the Asian twist succeeds in delighting our palates.

Serves 4

Burgers:

1¼ pounds salmon fillets, skin removed

3 quarter-size coins fresh ginger, peeled, smashed, and minced

¼ cup snipped fresh chives

2 tablespoons minced fresh purple basil or cilantro

grated zest of ½ navel orange

pinch of salt

pinch of sugar

1 tablespoon Asian fish sauce (*nam pla*), optional

cornmeal

Sauce:

¼ cup light mayonnaise, preferably Hellmann's or Best's

2 tablespoons frozen orange juice concentrate, thawed

1 teaspoon wasabi paste (tube or reconstituted powder)

4 sesame hamburger buns, grilled

watercress

paper-thin cucumber slices

In a food processor, pulse to combine the salmon, ginger, chives, basil, orange zest, salt, sugar, and fish sauce. The consistency of ground meat, not a paste, is the goal. Turn the salmon mixture out onto a cutting board and, with wet fingers, shape it into 4 patties. Dust the surface lightly with cornmeal and refrigerate for about 20 minutes to firm.

Combine the sauce ingredients and set aside.

Grill the salmon burgers for 3 to 4 minutes on an indoor lidded electric or stove-top grill or about 2 minutes per side over a white-ash charcoal fire. Serve immediately on grilled sesame buns lined with watercress and overlapping slices of cucumber. Top each burger with a spoonful of the mayonnaise sauce.

● **nutritional breakdown (per serving)**

Calories: 295	Carbohydrates: 7 g	Protein: 24 g	Fat: 18 g
Saturated fat: 4 g	% calories from fat: 55%	Cholesterol: 72 mg	Sodium: 215 mg

● **(with sesame bun)**

Calories: 424	Carbohydrates: 29 g	Protein: 28 g	Fat: 21 g
Saturated fat: 4 g	% calories from fat: 44%	Cholesterol: 72 mg	Sodium: 456 mg

Open-Face Catfish Burger

People who have an aversion to fish often love crab cakes, and kids love anything faintly resembling a burger. This recipe should win over both. The precooked fish fillets take on the texture of crab, and although we won't commit the heresy of suggesting they taste the same, this is not a beggar's version. It's simple, tasty, and the presentation beats the usual humdrum fish dinner. The burger would be equally appealing without the bun, served with coleslaw vinaigrette and crispy shoestring potatoes.

Serves 4

1 pound catfish fillets
1 large egg, beaten
1 tablespoon light mayonnaise, preferably Hellmann's or Best's
6 scallions, white part minced with ½ inch of the green
2 tablespoons minced celery
2 tablespoons minced red bell pepper
pinch of salt
⅛ teaspoon cayenne
⅓ cup crushed oyster crackers
cornmeal

2½ tablespoons Creole mustard
1½ tablespoons light sour cream

4 hamburger buns
leaf lettuce
1 large tomato, thinly sliced

Lay the fillets side by side in a microwave-safe dish, folding the tail ends under, and drizzle with 2 or 3 tablespoons of water. Cover with plastic wrap and cook on high for 2 minutes. Remove the cover and check to see if the fish is thoroughly cooked at its thick center. If it breaks apart easily with the side of a fork, it's done. If not, re-cover and return it to the microwave for 1-minute intervals. Remove the fillets to a layer of paper towels to drain and cool.

Whisk the egg in a medium bowl and add the mayonnaise, scallions, celery, pepper, salt, cayenne, and cracker crumbs. Stir to combine. With your fingers, gently flake the fish into the mixture, letting it fall in small enough pieces so that the patties will hold together, but avoid crushing the flakes. In other words, pretend you're making crab cakes.

Divide the mixture into 4 large balls, pressing it together gently. Sprinkle some cornmeal on a cutting board or plate and roll the balls in it, coating them lightly. Press the balls into fat patties and refrigerate for an hour to set the coating.

Combine the mustard and sour cream and set aside.

If you're using an indoor grill with a lid, it will take only about 3 minutes to heat the burgers thoroughly and set the binding. On a stovetop or outdoor grill, it will take about 5 minutes altogether. Meanwhile, toast the buns if you like.

Serve each burger on a half bun lined with a lettuce leaf and a thin slice of tomato. Put a dollop of mustard cream on top of each burger. Use the bun tops or not, as you prefer.

- **nutritional breakdown (per serving)**

| Calories: 238 | Carbohydrates: 11 g | Protein: 21 g | Fat: 12 g |
| Saturated fat: 3 g | % calories from fat: 46% | Cholesterol: 115 mg | Sodium: 377 mg |

- **(on ½ bun)**

| Calories: 299 | Carbohydrates: 21 g | Protein: 23 g | Fat: 13 g |
| Saturated fat: 3 g | % calories from fat: 40% | Cholesterol: 115 mg | Sodium: 498 mg |

Red, White, and Blue Buffalo Burger

This is the all-American burger of the new millennium, and it's very good! It's not surprising that it tastes much like beef, since buffalo and cattle have similar palates and are indigenous to the same environment. The culinary difference is that buffalo contains half the fat of beef, and with so little to protect the surface, ground buffalo can char before it reaches medium-rare or rare. That's just fine for steak, but we prefer our burgers with a less crunchy crust. If you disagree, by all means cook these burgers over high heat as you do beef—just keep them rare. The optional bacon strip protects the edges of the burger on an open fire and the top and bottom of the patties on an indoor grill. If you're avoiding extra calories, simply discard the bacon after it has served its purpose. We feel the low-fat buffalo gives us permission to relish a bacon cheeseburger once in a while. The sharp quality of blue cheese is a zesty contrast to the sweet, dense meat, and slivered tomato adds the counterpoint of flavor and color.

Serves 4

½ large red onion
1 pound ground buffalo
salt and freshly ground black pepper to taste
2 ounces low-fat cream cheese
1 ounce Maytag blue cheese
2 teaspoons soft unsalted butter
1 ripe tomato
4 thick slices lean smoky bacon
romaine lettuce leaves
4 hamburger buns

Mince the onion in a food processor or by hand and spread out on a cutting board. Distribute the ground meat over the onion. Season lightly with salt and pepper. With wet fingers, separate the clumps of meat while combining it thoroughly with the onion. Shape into 4 patties and set aside for grilling.

Mash the cream cheese, blue cheese, and butter together with a fork and divide into 4 knobs. Stem the tomato and cut it in half. Scoop out the pulp and seeds and sliver the shell. Set aside with the cheese mixture.

If cooking over charcoal, secure a strip of bacon around the edge of the burgers with a water-soaked toothpick. If cooking indoors, cut the bacon strip in half and put one half diagonally across the side facing down to moisten the meat as it cooks.

Grill the burgers over medium heat on a charcoal, stovetop, or electric grill for 3 to 4 minutes per side or on a lidded electric grill for 5 minutes altogether. Do not cook beyond medium-rare or the meat will become dry and unsavory.

Serve the burgers on lettuce-lined grilled buns with a knob of cheese on top and a sprinkling of tomato slivers.

nutritional breakdown (per serving)

| Calories: 262 | Carbohydrates: 4 g | Protein: 33 g | Fat: 12 g |
| Saturated fat: 6 g | % calories from fat: 40% | Cholesterol: 104 mg | Sodium: 560 mg |

(with bun)

| Calories: 385 | Carbohydrates: 26 g | Protein: 36 g | Fat: 14 g |
| Saturated fat: 7 g | % calories from fat: 32% | Cholesterol: 104 mg | Sodium: 801 mg |

Apple and Shiitake Venison Burger

This burger is a divine revelation. We urge you to try it whether you think you like venison or not. The ground venison now available in health food and specialty stores comes frozen in heavy vacuum-sealed pouches for perfect freshness. Because these deer are raised for meat production and are not wild, there is no gamy taste whatsoever. Perhaps that's a disadvantage for aficionados, but it makes this nutritious low-fat meat more appealing—especially to those with a Bambi complex. Since venison is so lean, it requires slightly lower heat to keep the surface from charring before it's cooked, even to medium-rare. The moist apples in this recipe act as interior protection against drying out, but be careful. If the meat turns gray inside, it's overcooked.

Serves 4

½ cup dried apple slices
fruity red wine or apple juice to cover
1½ tablespoons unsalted butter
1½ cups minced shiitake mushrooms
6 scallions, trimmed and minced
1 tablespoon fresh thyme leaves
¼ teaspoon ground mace
salt and freshly ground black pepper to taste
1 package (12 ounces) ground venison
pumpernickel or rye bread or hamburger buns
bottled horseradish cream

In a small bowl, cover the dried apples with the wine and put aside to soak.

Heat the butter in a medium skillet over medium-high heat and add the mushrooms and scallions. Stir until wilted and add the thyme, mace, and salt and pepper. If the mixture sticks to the pan, add a touch more butter. Sauté for about 5 minutes and remove from the heat.

When the apples are completely soft, squeeze the slices gently over the bowl to remove the excess liquid, then mince them on a cutting board. Fluff the ground meat over the apples and distribute the mushroom mixture on top. Drizzle a little of the wine soaking liquid over the surface to assure a moist burger. With your fingers, lightly and thoroughly combine the ingredients without compacting the meat.

Grill the burgers on a stovetop, electric, or white-ash charcoal grill for about 3 minutes per side or on a lidded electric grill for about 5 minutes altogether.

Serve them on untoasted bread or buns with horseradish cream.

cook's note: Packaged root chips go well with these burgers, but homemade celeriac chips relate even better to this deserving burger. They can be made easily and quickly by slicing a peeled and trimmed celery root with a vegetable peeler and dropping the paper-thin slices into hot canola oil for only a few minutes, until golden brown. They keep well and can be made ahead. Try mixing them with parsnip slices prepared in the same manner.

- **nutritional breakdown (per serving)**

| Calories: 209 | Carbohydrates: 14 g | Protein: 23 g | Fat: 7 g |
| Saturated fat: 4 g | % calories from fat: 30% | Cholesterol: 92 mg | Sodium: 245 mg |

- **(on 2 slices of pumpernickel)**

| Calories: 369 | Carbohydrates: 45 g | Protein: 28 g | Fat: 9 g |
| Saturated fat: 4 g | % calories from fat: 21% | Cholesterol: 92 mg | Sodium: 675 mg |

Mushroom, Barley, and Hazelnut Burgers

The similarity between this burger and others in this chapter ends with the shape of the patty. A meatless hamburger is an oxymoron, but there are those times when you're not in a high-protein mood. Or perhaps you invited vegetarian friends to dinner and are stymied over what to serve. This is a very tasty blend of familiar ingredients, with barley providing the substance and hazelnuts the crunch. The mixture can be made ahead and refrigerated, and it's much easier to shape chilled. The patties are a bit fragile, so if you want to grill them over an open fire, use a wire basket to hold them together when they're flipped. Since there is a fair amount of bread crumbs in the recipe, it's best to forgo the doughy hamburger bun in favor of light toast.

Serves 4 to 6

¾ pound mixed cremini, oyster, shiitake, and button mushrooms
½ cup whole hazelnuts
1½ cups fine bread crumbs
3 tablespoons unsalted butter
2 large shallots, minced
2 garlic cloves, smashed and minced
1 teaspoon dried thyme
salt and freshly ground black pepper to taste
pinch of cayenne
1 large egg
1 cup cooked instant barley, Quaker Oats Mother's brand
3 tablespoons minced parsley
⅓ cup grated Parmesan cheese
challah or brioche bread, toasted and buttered

Stem the mushrooms. Wipe off any surface dirt with a damp sponge or towel. Mince them in a food processor and set aside.

Preheat the oven to 300°. Rub the skins from the hazelnuts in a clean tea towel. Toast them in the oven for about 5 minutes, or until fragrant and light golden brown. Leave the oven on and toast the bread crumbs about 5 minutes, or until light golden brown. When the nuts are cool, chop by hand or pulse in a food processor. Set both aside.

Melt the butter in a large sauté pan or wok. Add the shallots, garlic, thyme, salt and pepper, and cayenne. When the shallots are soft, add the mushrooms and combine. Sauté about 5 minutes, or until the mushrooms have wilted. Remove from the heat and cool. Gently blot the surface moisture with a paper towel.

Whisk the egg in a large bowl. Add the barley, parsley, cheese, nuts, 1 cup of the bread crumbs, and all the mushrooms. Combine well. Taste for seasoning and adjust. Chill thoroughly or refrigerate, uncovered, for as long as 2 or 3 days.

Form the mixture into 6 or 8 patties, pressing together firmly. Roll in the remaining ½ cup bread crumbs to lightly coat the surface. Grill simply to heat. Serve open-face on buttered, toasted challah.

cook's notes: Use this same mixutre to make small *polpette,* or meatballs. Shape it into 2-inch balls, coat them in crumbs, sauté until golden, and then serve over fettuccine with a lemony cream sauce brightened with minced parsley.

nutritional breakdown (per serving for 4)

Calories: 238	Carbohydrates: 11 g	Protein: 21 g	Fat: 12 g
Saturated fat: 3 g	% calories from fat: 46%	Cholesterol: 115 mg	Sodium: 377 mg

(on ½ bun)

Calories: 299	Carbohydrates: 21 g	Protein: 23 g	Fat: 13 g
Saturated fat: 3 g	% calories from fat: 40%	Cholesterol: 115 mg	Sodium: 498 mg

Grilled Pizza

Grilled pizza? You bet—and it's delicious. Grilled over charcoal, pizza takes on an earthy flavor that transforms it into something bearing no resemblance to the pitiful pie often delivered to your front door. Achieving good results over an open flame requires a medium-hot fire well banked to one side, with a section of the grill left open for indirect baking. The more easily regulated gas grill makes the back and forth shift in heat intensity simpler, but the smoky taste of wood or charcoal will be lost. No indoor grill without a cover can do this job, but we were awed to discover that our indoor/outdoor electric grill with a heavy dome-shaped lid delivered a crispy crust and perfectly melted cheese. Best of all, the kitchen stayed cool.

Tips for Grilling Pizza

- Find a good Italian market or independent pizza shop that makes and sells fresh pizza dough daily. It makes a teriffic pie in the shortest time and with the least fuss. Prebaked supermarket shells on the grill are pointless. When time isn't an issue and if dough making does not intimidate you, prepare your own favorite pizza dough recipe.

- Allow refrigerated store-bought dough to come to room temperature before stretching it into shape.

- Stretch, don't roll, the dough into one large or two smaller rounds, and don't worry if your circle looks more like a puddle. Free-form edges are appropriately rustic. Just keep the center as thin as possible, short of tearing holes in the dough. The rim should be only slightly thicker to keep toppings from running away. You can cut short sticks of cheese and roll the rim around them if you tend to leave a plain edge on your plate.

- Pizza dough resists being stretched into shape and tends to fight back with frustrating persistence. Whenever it gets sassy, give it a brief time-out.

- Lacking a humongous wooden peel, shape your pie(s) on a rimless cookie pan sprinkled liberally with cornmeal or grits so the pizza will slide right off onto the grill.

- Have the toppings prepared and on a tray next to the grill. Once the dough is ready, you should move quickly. Keep a bottle of extra-virgin olive oil and a dish of coarse salt nearby as well. You can use tongs to flip the crust.

- Don't return the cookie pan to the kitchen; you'll need it to slide the finished pizza onto and carry it to a cutting board. You'll risk ruining both knife and cookie pan attempting to cut it on the metal. If you're a dedicated pizza maker, invest in a commercial-weight wheel cutter, available in gourmet equipment stores and restaurant supply houses.

Outdoor Grilling

Build a hot hardwood-charcoal fire to one or both sides of the grill, leaving enough unheated room either way to slide the crust(s) back and forth as needed. Slide the dough first onto the hot side of the grill and drop the lid down, and within about 3 minutes, you'll see the dough release puffed bubbles and stiffen. When obvious grill marks appear, pull the pizza off onto the cookie pan, cooked side up. Adjust your fire to medium by spreading the coals out and letting them burn down a bit. A spray bottle of water can accomplish this quickly. In the few minutes this takes, lightly brush the grilled surface of the pizza, including the rim, with olive oil and sprinkle with salt. Add the toppings of your choice. Slide the pizza back over the heat and lower the lid. The pizza is done when the cheese is bubbling and the edges are appealingly charred but not burned. This back and forth, up and down heat routine serves the purpose of assuring that the center of the dough is thoroughly cooked at the same time both surfaces are sealed and crispy. If your pizza has a doughy center, you need to practice again. It's a lot of fun, and what a heavenly perfume fills the air and permeates the pizza. You'll be hooked.

Indoor Grilling .

If you have one of those indoor/outdoor dome-lidded grills, you can make a very respectable pizza. The only real advantages over baking it in a blistering hot oven are that you can avoid heating up your kitchen and you can roll your grill out onto the patio or balcony and avoid racing back and forth to see if the pizza is done. Besides, there's something kind of nice about baking a pizza outdoors, wood fire or not.

The cooking procedure is the same as given above for charcoal grilling. You cannot, however, work with zoned heat. Preheat your grill to its hottest temperature for round one, and while you're layering the toppings, reduce the thermostat to the low end of the red zone to finish it off. The lid should be down throughout.

Roasted Eggplant and Peppers

1 large eggplant
1 red and 1 yellow roasted pepper, chopped
salt and freshly ground black pepper to taste
1 tablespoon extra-virgin olive oil
1 tablespoon minced onion
1 tablespoon chopped Spanish capers

2 tablespoons tomato puree

¼ cup chopped flat-leaf parsley

2 garlic cloves

crumbled Greek feta cheese

Roast or grill the whole eggplant until it's tender but not collapsed. Slit it open, remove the flesh, and chop it coarsely. Combine it with the rest of the ingredients except the cheese, pressing the garlic through a press into the mixture. Spread the mixture on the grilled side of the pizza crust and sprinkle the feta cheese on top.

● **nutritional breakdown (per serving of ⅛ of a pie)**

Calories: 727	Carbohydrates: 123 g	Protein: 21 g	Fat: 17 g
Saturated fat: 6 g	% calories from fat: 21%	Cholesterol: 25 mg	Sodium: 801 mg

Charred Red and White Onions with Prosciutto and Black Walnuts

1 medium red onion, sliced ½ inch thick

1 medium white or sweet onion, sliced ½ inch thick

superfine sugar

salt and freshly ground black pepper to taste

3 thin slices prosciutto

⅓ cup black walnuts (2.25-ounce package), chopped

3 garlic cloves, crushed and minced

1½ tablespoons soy sauce

2 tablespoons sherry vinegar

2 to 3 tablespoons walnut oil

grated Parmigiano-Reggiano cheese

Sprinkle the onions very lightly with superfine sugar and char them on an indoor or outdoor grill until soft and speckled with black. Season them with salt and pepper.

Crisp the prosciutto on the grill and tear it into strips. Combine with the rest of the ingredients except the cheese and spread on the grilled side of the pizza crust. Cover with the cheese.

nutritional breakdown (per serving ⅕ of a pie)

Calories: 774	Carbohydrates: 113 g	Protein: 24 g	Fat: 25 g
Saturated fat: 3 g	% calories from fat: 29%	Cholesterol: 9 mg	Sodium: 1,029 mg

Roasted Garlic, Baby Spinach, and Grape Tomatoes

1 head garlic, roasted (see page 127)
2 teaspoons extra-virgin olive oil
salt and freshly ground black pepper to taste
6 ounces fresh mozzarella, thinly sliced
1 bag fresh baby spinach
½ cup slivered grape tomatoes
2 tablespoons pine nuts, toasted
grated Parmigiano-Reggiano cheese

Squeeze the roasted garlic pulp into the oil and make a paste. Season with salt and pepper and spread the mixture over the grilled side of the crust. Top with the mozzarella. Lay the spinach leaves out over the cheese, scatter the tomato slivers around, and sprinkle the pine nuts and cheese on top.

● **nutritional breakdown (per serving ⅛ of a pie)**

Calories: 759	Carbohydrates: 110g	Protein: 27 g	Fat: 22 g
Saturated fat: 8 g	% calories from fat: 26%	Cholesterol: 37 mg	Sodium: 578 mg

White Pizza Portobello

Thinly slice portobello mushrooms and marinate them for at least 20 minutes in olive oil seasoned with minced fresh herbs (oregano, rosemary, thyme, parlsey), minced garlic, and salt and pepper. Line the grilled side of the crust with grated Fontina and fresh mozzarella cheese and top with the marinated mushrooms.

● **nutritional breakdown (per serving of ⅛ of a pie)**

Calories: 792	Carbohydrates: 109 g	Protein: 29 g	Fat: 25 g
Saturated fat: 11 g	% calories from fat: 28%	Cholesterol: 54 mg	Sodium: 636 mg

Vegetables and Salads

Bisteca Insalata

Lamb Kabobs with Country Salad

Glazed Chicken over Spinach Salad

Chicken Sausage and Grilled Potato Salad

Chicken Panzanella

Carol's Tropical Turkey Salad

Prosciutto-Wrapped Shrimp with Lemony White Bean Salad

Watercress and Cucumber with Fresh Tuna

Penne with Leeks, Radicchio, and Artichokes

Spaghetti Verdure

Mixed Mushroom Fettuccine

A Few More Vegetable Ideas

Bisteca Insalata

This combination is such a welcome change from steak and potatoes. It makes a refreshing full meal out of one generous steak without giving that way-too-much, uncomfortably full feeling red meat can sometimes inflict. Select a top-quality, tender cut of meat for this salad. You're going to need only one steak, and if it isn't juicy and delicious, this salad will quickly lose its charm. Serve this with heated ciabatta bread or tomato focaccia from your local bakery.

Serves 4

1 porterhouse steak, at least 1¼ inches thick
salt and freshly ground black pepper to taste

Salad Dressing:
3 garlic cloves, smashed and minced
4 flat anchovies, optional
6 tablespoons extra-virgin olive oil
2 tablespoons fresh lemon juice
½ teaspoon Worcestershire sauce
pinch of salt, if anchovies are not used
freshly ground black pepper to taste

Salad:
mixed greens: mesclun, baby spinach, radicchio, arugula,
   red leaf lettuce
1 fennel bulb, trimmed and cut in thin slivers
2 yellow tomatoes, cut in eighths
6 scallions, trimmed and slivered
¼ cup capers

Parmigiano-Reggiano cheese

Season the steak with salt and pepper and set aside.

Combine all the salad dressing ingredients in a screw-top jar. Shake vigorously and set aside. Have the salad ingredients prepared and ready for tossing.

Sear the steak on both sides on a stovetop, electric, or outdoor grill. Continue cooking for another 3 to 4 minutes per side. If you are using a lidded electric grill, it's better to cut the meat from the bone before grilling to be sure that the meat hits the grill surface evenly. In all instances, an instant-read thermometer should register 115° to 120° for a rare steak. Let the steak rest for 5 minutes before slicing. Slice it thinly in wide strips and then again lengthwise into thin strips that can easily be eaten without further cutting.

Assemble the salad in a large bowl, add the steak strips, and toss with the dressing. Using a vegetable peeler, peel several paper-thin shards of cheese from the chunk of Parmigiano-Reggiano and garnish the salad with them.

● **nutritional breakdown (per serving)**

Calories: 518	Carbohydrates: 13 g	Protein: 22 g	Fat: 43 g
Saturated fat: 11 g	% calories from fat: 74%	Cholesterol: 64 mg	Sodium: 514 mg

Lamb Kabobs with Country Salad

W e do tend to fall into familiar roles when we cook out. One person always gets the solo grill duty, and another solo kitchen duty, and if there's a young errand runner around, he or she gets to sprint back and forth from kitchen to grill with cold drinks and all things forgotten. Here's a complete meal idea that allows everyone to be outside toasting the sizzling kabobs. If you're grilling indoors, you can even do it tableside. The lamb takes mere minutes to cook, and the sturdy salad won't suffer a bit from waiting.

Serves 4

1 pound loin lamb cubes

Marinade:

¼ cup extra-virgin olive oil

4 garlic cloves, smashed and minced

1 teaspoon dried oregano, preferably Greek

2 tablespoons fresh lemon juice

coarse salt and freshly ground black pepper to taste

Salad:

1 head romaine lettuce, torn in chunks

2 dead-ripe tomatoes, quartered

1 green bell pepper, stemmed, seeded, and cut in thin strips

½ red onion, thinly sliced

1 cucumber, peeled, seeded, and cut into thick slices

8 to 12 Kalamata olives, pitted

6 ounces Greek feta cheese, crumbled

1 tablespoon fresh thyme leaves

salt and freshly ground black pepper to taste

Salad Dressing:

2 garlic cloves, smashed and minced

1 teaspoon Dijon mustard

pinch of salt

6 tablespoons extra-virgin olive oil

2 tablespoons red wine vinegar

Put the lamb cubes in a plastic storage bag. Whisk together the marinade ingredients and pour over the lamb. Seal the bag and store overnight in the refrigerator.

Assemble and prepare the vegetables for the salad. Combine the dressing ingredients in a screw-top jar and set aside. Soak wooden skewers in water for about 30 minutes if you are cooking outdoors.

Divide the lamb into even portions, saving the marinade for basting. Slide the cubes onto 8 short skewers and season with salt and pepper. Cook the kabobs on a stovetop, electric, or outdoor grill for 3 to 4 minutes per side, basting when you turn them. They should take no longer than 5 minutes altogether in a lidded electric grill. Use the thumb test described on page 24 to check for doneness.

Put all the salad ingredients in a large salad bowl, season with salt and pepper, and toss with the dressing. Serve each plate with a mound of salad in the center and a kabob on either side.

nutritional breakdown (per serving)

Calories: 690	Carbohydrates: 15 g	Protein: 31 g	Fat: 58 g
Saturated fat: 19 g	% calories from fat: 75%	Cholesterol: 122 mg	Sodium: 949 mg

Glazed Chicken over Spinach Salad

Often contemporary cooking is nothing more than a simple upgrade of an old favorite—an improvement in the quality and convenience of ingredients, a reduction in richness in payment for past indulgences, or a bright flourish or two to keep us interested. California was the first to introduce flat-leaf spinach, and what an improvement over the gritty, crinkly kind that made salad making a chore and a half. Now we have triple-washed baby spinach with tender edible stems and without whatever it was in the tough old stuff that made our teeth squeak. We've added red leaf lettuce to the spinach and, defying tradition, tossed it with a more svelte blue cheese dressing. The balsamic glazed chicken is a perfect foil for the tart dressing, and the dried cranberries accentuate the vinegar's sweet edge.

Serves 4

1 pound chicken tenders or boneless chicken breasts
canola oil
salt and freshly ground black pepper to taste
3 tablespoons balsamic vinegar
1 teaspoon light brown sugar

Salad Dressing:
¾ cup plain low-fat yogurt
¼ cup crumbled blue cheese
2 garlic cloves, pressed through garlic press
2 tablespoons snipped fresh chives
salt and freshly ground black pepper to taste

Salad:

baby spinach or regular flat-leaf, mixed 2 to 1 with red leaf lettuce

yellow grape tomatoes, or 2 yellow tomato shells, slivered

2 tablespoons Craisins

1 tablespoon pine nuts, toasted

If you're cooking outdoors, soak 8 to 12 wooden skewers in water for at least 30 minutes. If you're using boneless chicken breasts, pull off the tender underneath and pound the breast flat between 2 pieces of plastic wrap. Cut the meat into strips the same width as the tenders. Thread the skewers in and out of the meat in a running-stitch fashion and push the meat close together in loops. Brush the chicken lightly with oil and season with salt and pepper.

Combine the vinegar and brown sugar in a small dish and set aside with a basting brush.

For the dressing, put the yogurt and blue cheese in a food processor. Add the garlic and pulse until the dressing is smooth. If it seems too thick, thin it with a little canola oil but keep in mind that it will thin out a little when tossed with the moist lettuce. Fold in the snipped chives and season with a pinch of salt and some pepper. Taste and adjust if necessary.

Cook the skewered chicken on a stovetop, electric, or outdoor grill for 1 to 2 minutes per side, glazing with the vinegar mixture on both sides during the last few seconds. On a lidded electric grill with the top down, the chicken will take only about 3 minutes altogether. Lift the lid, brush with the vinegar, and lower the lid just long enough to caramelize the glaze.

Toss the greens with the dressing and grape tomatoes. Sprinkle the top with the dried cranberries and pine nuts. Mound the salad onto a platter and surround the salad with the chicken skewers.

● **nutritional breakdown (per serving)**

Calories: 285	Carbohydrates: 13 g	Protein: 33 g	Fat: 11 g
Saturated fat: 3 g	% calories from fat: 34%	Cholesterol: 81 mg	Sodium: 568 mg

Chicken Sausage and Grilled Potato Salad

Whether made of chicken, turkey, or pork, sausage is great on the grill, so why not grill its classic accompaniment, potato salad with a zesty mustard vinaigrette? This is a welcome change from the usual weekday supper and is about as simple as it can be. Either chicken sausage with apple or lemon sausage would be a good choice for this potato salad.

Serves 4 to 6

2 pounds Yukon Gold or Red Bliss potatoes

1 sweet onion, peeled and quartered

6 to 8 chicken sausages

½ cup canned low-sodium chicken broth

salt and freshly ground black pepper to taste

2 tablespoons Dijon mustard with horseradish

2 tablespoons rice vinegar or cider vinegar

6 tablespoons extra-virgin olive oil

2 tablespoons minced flat-leaf parsley

1½ tablespoons minced fresh thyme

If you are using Yukon Gold potatoes, peel them and cut them in half lengthwise. If you are using Red Bliss, scrub them and cut them across. If you are cooking over an open fire, oil the potatoes lightly and grill over medium heat for 30 to 40 minutes, or until they are tender. If you are cooking indoors, steam the potatoes in the microwave, covered, in a small amount of water for 5 minutes on high. Pat them dry, oil them lightly, and put them on a stovetop or electric grill until tender throughout and crusty on the cut edge.

Lightly oil the onion quarters and grill them indoors or out until soft and slightly charred. The sausages can go on the grill at the same time.

Heat the chicken broth. Cut the potatoes into a bowl and pour the broth over them. Season with salt and pepper. Set aside.

Whisk together the rest of the ingredients and pour over the potatoes. Chop the grilled onion and fold in. Taste for seasoning.

Serve the potato salad slightly warm along with the grilled sausages.

● **nutritional breakdown (per serving for 4)**

Calories: 575	Carbohydrates: 45 g	Protein: 22 g	Fat: 35 g
Saturated fat: 7 g	% calories from fat: 55%	Cholesterol: 98 mg	Sodium: 757 mg

Chicken Panzanella

When the summer sun makes tomato vines run amok and bend to their knees from the weight of their juicy red cargo, we start wondering how to serve tomatoes for breakfast. We haven't solved that one yet, but remembering the sublime flavor of an Italian panzanella—good country bread sopping up sweet ruby tomatoes and their juices—we thought it would be a superb partner for grilled chicken. It is worth grilling a few extra chicken parts when you make Pollo Diavolo (page 80) so you can enjoy panzanella a few days later. Or surely there's chicken left over from grilling a whole one on the rotisserie.

Serves 4

Salad:

8 thick slices bakery rustic bread or focaccia

3 dead-ripe farm stand tomatoes

½ medium red onion

1 ball (8 ounces) fresh mozzarella, water-packed

2 tablespoons capers

1 roasted red pepper, torn into strips

1½ cups shredded grilled chicken

⅓ cup slivered fresh basil leaves

¼ cup minced flat-leaf parsley

salt and freshly ground black pepper to taste

Dressing:

½ cup extra-virgin olive oil

3 tablespoons red wine vinegar

1 tablespoon balsamic vinegar

Be sure you have selected a peasant bread with some substance, or this salad will be soggy and unpleasant. Tear the bread into a large salad bowl in big bite-size chunks.

Stem the tomatoes and, holding them over the bowl, gently squeeze their juices over the bread. Still working over the bread, quarter the tomatoes and cut each quarter into small pieces. Toss to combine.

Slice the onion as thinly as possible. Stack the slices and chop through them several times. Add to the bread salad. Cube the mozzarella or, if it's too soft to cut, shred it with your fingers. Add to the bowl along with the rest of the salad ingredients except the salt and pepper.

Whisk together the dressing ingredients and pour over the salad. Season generously with salt and pepper and toss. Taste and adjust the seasonings.

● **nutritional breakdown (per serving)**

Calories: 675	Carbohydrates: 39 g	Protein: 33 g	Fat: 43 g
Saturated fat: 12 g	% calories from fat: 57%	Cholesterol: 89 mg	Sodium: 738 mg

Carol's Tropical Turkey Salad

Have you ever wanted to lick your plate? Once you taste this salad, we bet you'll carry your own plate to the kitchen just so you can get away with it. You should also check to see that there's film in your camera, because the sheer visual impact of the ingredients vies for top billing with their exotic flavors. Try this special salad with leftovers from Smoky Maple Rum Turkey on page 106 or Spicy Lime and Cilantro Chicken on page 84.

Serves 4

Salad Dressing:

¼ cup mango chutney

1 teaspoon grated fresh ginger

½ teaspoon salt

⅛ teaspoon Pico de Gallo (see Cook's Note, page 61), or cayenne to taste

¼ cup raspberry vinegar

2 teaspoons fresh lime juice

2 teaspoons pure peanut oil, preferably marked "fragrant"

¾ cup canola oil

Salad:

12 shiitake mushrooms, stemmed

1 head romaine lettuce, trimmed

salt and freshly ground black pepper to taste

1 canned or bottled roasted red pepper, cut in strips

1 large ripe papaya, peeled, seeded, and cut in strips

2 ripe mangoes, peeled, pitted, and cut in strips

½ ripe avocado, peeled, pitted, and sliced

12 ounces cooked turkey breast, cut in strips

ombine the dressing ingredients in a food processor. The dressing will be thick and may look slightly separated. Scrape it into a bowl and whisk it into a smooth but textured emulsion.

Grill or sauté the shiitakes until they are just tender. Cut them in half and set aside.

Tear the romaine into bite-size pieces and line a serving platter or individual plates. Season the lettuce with salt and pepper. Arrange all of the salad ingredients in an attractive manner and drizzle the dressing over the top.

nutritional breakdown (per serving)

Calories: 715	Carbohydrates: 47 g	Protein: 30 g	Fat: 48 g
Saturated fat: 4 g	% calories from fat: 60%	Cholesterol: 71 mg	Sodium: 498 mg

Prosciutto-Wrapped Shrimp with Lemony White Bean Salad

Shrimp and prosciutto are a lovely combination; alone, each would make a great addition to a cocktail buffet. Here the ham protects the shrimp from drying out and takes on a crispy quality when it's grilled. Combining the shrimp with white beans dressed with a lemon and herb vinaigrette transforms them into a delicious summer main dish. Serve it along with a platter of sliced farm stand tomatoes and fresh mozzarella drizzled with fruity olive oil.

Serves 4

1 pound large shrimp, shelled and deveined
salt and freshly ground black pepper to taste
6 paper-thin slices prosciutto
extra-virgin olive oil, preferably in a mister or spray can

Salad:

2 cans (15 ounces each) white beans, cannellini, or Great Northern
  beans, rinsed and drained
4 garlic cloves, pressed
3 tablespoons minced scallions, white part only
2 tablespoons minced flat-leaf parsley
1 tablespoon each minced fresh mint and basil
3 tablespoons extra-virgin olive oil
1 tablespoon fresh lemon juice
salt and freshly ground black pepper to taste
arugula for garnish, optional

Pat the shrimp very dry and season them lightly with salt and pepper. Cut the prosciutto in thin strips without removing the fat; it will melt off quickly when grilled. Don't worry if the strips are ragged. Wind a strip around each shrimp in a single layer, using half a strip if that does the job. Leave about ½ inch uncovered at the head end of the shrimp so you can check for doneness. The ham should stick to itself, but you can use a toothpick on the stubborn ones; just pull it out when you turn the shrimp. Spray or lightly brush the shrimp with olive oil.

If you are cooking on an outdoor grill or in an electric rotisserie, fit the shrimp into a basket to facilitate turning them and to make it easier to pull them away from a possible flare-up.

Combine all the salad ingredients except the arugula but do not refrigerate if you're serving within a few hours. The beans should be served at room temperature.

Cook the shrimp on a stovetop, electric, or outdoor grill for about 2 minutes per side, depending on the size of the shrimp. Check the exposed end to see if the flesh is opaque and use the thumb test described on page 24.

Mound the bean salad on a large platter and encircle it with the arugula. Nestle the shrimp on the greens.

● **nutritional breakdown (per serving)**

Calories: 384	Carbohydrates: 31 g	Protein: 32 g	Fat: 14 g
Saturated fat: 2 g	% calories from fat: 32%	Cholesterol: 189 mg	Sodium: 1,233 mg

Watercress and Cucumber with Fresh Tuna

This is not really a main-dish salad, unless you are planning a light lunch. It is, however, a splendid company appetizer, perfect before Ponzu Cornish Hen with Shiitake (page 96), or a simple rotisserie chicken, so we decided to pass it along. You can also make a great leftover chicken or turkey salad with this dressing, adding crisp celery, grated carrot, and slivered scallions.

Serves 4

1 yellowtail tuna steak, 1 inch thick

canola or peanut oil

salt and freshly ground black pepper to taste

Salad Dressing:

1½ teaspoons Dijon mustard

½ teaspoon grated fresh ginger, with the juice

½ teaspoon sugar

pinch of salt

1 garlic clove, pressed

1 tablespoon hoisin sauce

1 tablespoon reduced-sodium soy sauce

1 teaspoon fresh lime juice

1 teaspoon fragrant or cold-pressed peanut oil

3 tablespoons canola oil

Salad:

> 2 bunches watercress, stemmed
>
> 1 tablespoon grated carrot
>
> 1 large cucumber, halved lengthwise, seeded, and sliced ¼ inch thick
>
> daikon radish for garnish, optional

Brush the tuna steak lightly with oil and season with salt and pepper.

Whisk to combine the salad dressing ingredients or shake in a screw-top jar. Set aside.

Wash, stem, and spin-dry the watercress. Toss with the grated carrot and refrigerate in a bowl. Store the cucumber slices separately. If you have the daikon, scrape it like a carrot and then peel off strips about 1 inch wide with your vegetable peeler. Drop the strips into a small bowl filled with water and a few ice cubes. Refrigerate. The strips will curl up when thoroughly cold.

Quickly sear the fish on both sides on a stovetop, electric, or outdoor grill. This will take a minute on each side. Check for doneness at 30-second intervals, keeping in mind that the tuna will cook further between the heat and the plate. The inside should be grayish pink with a ½-inch translucent red stripe in the center. Do not overcook or the tuna will be hopelessly dry and tasteless.

Slice the fish thinly. No need to rush—this is a cool dish. Divide the slices into portions and lay them out on individual plates in an overlapping fan. Mound the watercress and carrot next to the fish and the cucumber around the base. Drizzle the dressing over the tuna and greens. Garnish with the daikon curls.

cook's notes: Salad preparation can be done way ahead of grilling time.

If you would like to turn this into a main dish, chop the watercress, cut the cucumber in tiny cubes, and toss them along with the carrot into a bowl of cooked and cooled rice noodles or angel hair pasta. Double the dressing recipe so you can coat the noodle salad. Arrange the tuna slices in spoke fashion under the mound of noodles and garnish with the daikon.

nutritional breakdown (per serving)

Calories: 256	Carbohydrates: 7 g	Protein: 19 g	Fat: 17 g
Saturated fat: 2 g	% calories from fat: 60%	Cholesterol: 40 mg	Sodium: 401 mg

Penne with Leeks, Radicchio, and Artichokes

We don't often think of outdoor cooking when we think of pasta, but you'd be surprised by how a simple pasta dinner can become quite special when the topping is flash-cooked over an open flame or on a searingly hot electric grill. A sturdy pasta like penne can be cooked ahead, oiled to prevent sticking, and reheated in a skillet on the side of an outdoor grill or on the stove.

Serves 4

¾ pound penne rigate

extra-virgin olive oil for coating pasta and vegetables

2 artichokes, trimmed, leaving 1 inch of stem, or frozen artichoke
    hearts, thawed

1 lemon, cut in half

salt and freshly ground black pepper to taste

3 leeks, washed and trimmed, leaving 1 inch of the green

1 head radicchio, cored

2 tablespoons extra-virgin olive oil

2 tablespoons unsalted butter

2 garlic cloves, smashed and minced

2 tablespoons slivered fresh sage

¼ cup minced flat-leaf parsley

12 Kalamata olives, pitted

¼ cup grated Parmigiano-Reggiano or aged Asiago cheese

Cook the penne in a large stockpot of rapidly boiling salted water until it is al dente. Reserving ¼ cup of the pasta water, drain the penne but don't rinse it. As soon as it has cooled a bit, pour a little olive oil in a cupped palm and run your fingers through the pasta to lightly coat it and prevent sticking.

If you're using fresh artichokes, cut off the top within an inch of the base and snap off the heavy outer leaves. Cut off the stem at the base and peel it with a vegetable peeler. Rub all cut edges with lemon to prevent darkening. If you have the patience to remove a raw choke, fine, but it will be far easier to remove after cooking. You can either partially cook the artichokes in rapidly boiling water for about 12 minutes or put them in a covered microwave-safe dish with ½ cup of water and steam them on high for 5 minutes.

If you're using frozen artichoke hearts, simply pat them completely dry, coat them lightly with olive oil, and season with salt and pepper.

Cut the leeks in half lengthwise. Slice the radicchio crosswise into thick strips. Rub or spray both vegetables lightly with olive oil and season with salt and pepper.

Grill the artichokes and leeks until they are tender when pierced with the tip of a knife and they have picked up attractive golden stripes. Put the radicchio on last and toss it around with tongs until it has charred slightly. Radicchio becomes sweeter when it's cooked.

Cut whole artichokes in quarters and scrape out the choke with the tip of a spoon. Chop the leeks roughly.

Heat the oil and butter in a wok or large sauté pan and add the garlic. Sauté until the garlic is soft but not brown. Add the penne and reheat. Add the vegetables, herbs, and olives and toss to combine. Drizzle in the reserved pasta water to moisten the dish. Serve piping hot with the grated cheese on top.

● **nutritional breakdown (per serving)**

Calories: 643	Carbohydrates: 89 g	Protein: 21 g	Fat: 24 g
Saturated fat: 7 g	% calories from fat: 33%	Cholesterol: 20 mg	Sodium: 696 mg

Spaghetti Verdure

Whether you grill them outdoors over a live flame or indoors on an electric grill, some vegetables develop a far more interesting character when exposed to direct heat. Their natural sugars caramelize, intensifing their flavor. They also look more appetizing with their golden stripes and lacy bits of char. We like arranging these striking vegetables on a plate of steaming pasta suggestive of a Tuscan trattoria.

Serves 4

1 eggplant, peeled and thickly sliced

coarse salt

¾ pound spaghetti

2 tablespoons extra-virgin olive oil

2 tablespoons unsalted butter

3 garlic cloves, pressed

¼ cup minced flat-leaf parsley

¼ cup thinly slivered fresh basil leaves

1 red bell pepper

1 yellow bell pepper

olive oil for coating vegetables

1 sweet onion, peeled and halved crosswise

4 plum tomatoes, stemmed

2 zucchini, halved crosswise

salt and freshly ground black pepper to taste

⅓ cup grated Parmigiano-Reggiano cheese

ine a cookie sheet with waxed paper and lay out the eggplant slices. Sprinkle the slices with coarse salt on both sides. Set aside.

In a large stockpot of boiling salted water, cook the spaghetti for 8 to 10 minutes, or until it is just al dente. Reserving ¼ cup of the pasta water, drain the spaghetti in a large colander. Heat the oil, butter, and garlic in a wok or large sauté pan and dump in the spaghetti. Remove the pan from the heat and lift and toss the pasta with tongs while adding the parsley and basil.

Rinse the salt and bitter juices from the eggplant and blot the slices dry. Core and seed the peppers and cut them into wide strips along their natural rib lines. Lightly oil all the vegetables and season with salt and pepper.

Grill the vegetables, starting with the onion and eggplant, until everything is just tender and the tomatoes have started to collapse. Everything can be successfully grilled either indoors or out over a medium-hot fire. Reheat the spaghetti on the edge of the grill or on the stove. Serve it on hot plates with the eggplant slices underneath and the other vegetables arranged on top. Pass the cheese separately.

● **nutritional breakdown (per serving)**

Calories: 575	Carbohydrates: 88 g	Protein: 19 g	Fat: 18 g
Saturated fat: 7 g	% calories from fat: 27%	Cholesterol: 23 mg	Sodium: 532 mg

Mixed Mushroom Fettuccine

So many varieties of wild mushrooms that were previously unavailable to most of us are now being grown commercially and sit beckoning in their market baskets. They may not have quite the flavor and romance of their more exotic woodland cousins, but they are wonderfully distinctive nonetheless. What to do with them? As little as possible. Toss them in a grill basket to be lightly smoked over hardwood charcoal or sear them quickly over an indoor grill. Serve them over a simply dressed pasta or over grilled polenta with cheese. A side dish of grilled asparagus (page 216) would be a sublime complement—a culinary ode to spring.

Serves 4

1 pound assorted mushrooms: shiitake, cremini, portobello, white button, oyster, chanterelle, porcini

extra-virgin olive oil for coating mushrooms

salt and freshly ground black pepper to taste

2 tablespoons extra-virgin olive oil

2 tablespoons unsalted butter

2 garlic cloves, smashed

¾ pound fresh fettuccine

2 tablespoons fresh lemon juice

2 tablespoons minced flat-leaf parsley

2 tablespoons snipped fresh chives

¼ cup grated Parmigiano-Reggiano cheese

Put a large stockpot of well-salted water on to boil.

Stem the shiitakes and portobellos completely and trim the stems of the rest. It's sufficient to wipe off any dirt with a damp paper towel. Resist soaking mushrooms in water; they soak up liquid like a sponge and will be impossible to sear. Spray or brush the mushrooms with olive oil and season them with salt and pepper. Cut very large mushrooms into bite-size pieces and leave smaller ones whole. They will shrink over the heat. If you are cooking outdoors, put them, caps down, in a grilling basket or over a fine screen.

Heat the olive oil and butter in a wok or a large sauté pan. Add the garlic, remove the wok from the burner, and allow the garlic to season the oil and butter.

Sear the mushrooms, caps down, on a stovetop, electric, or outdoor grill just until they pick up golden stripes and become slightly limp.

Drop the fettuccine into the rapidly boiling water. When a strand tests al dente, spoon out ¼ cup of the pasta water. Drain the fettuccine in a colander but don't rinse. Return the wok to the stove and quickly reheat the oil. Remove the garlic and add the lemon juice, herbs, and some salt and pepper. Turn the pasta into the wok and, with the heat on low, combine it well with the seasoned oil. Tongs make this a quick and simple operation. If the fettuccine seems at all dry, pour some of the reserved cooking water over it and toss. Add the cheese and toss again. Add more pasta water if needed. There should be no liquid in the bottom of the pan, and every strand of pasta should be coated with sauce and cheese.

Lift the pasta onto hot plates with tongs and top with the grilled mushrooms. Serve immediately. Guests wait for pasta—never vice versa.

● **nutritional breakdown (per serving)**

Calories: 466	Carbohydrates: 54 g	Protein: 16 g	Fat: 22 g
Saturated fat: 7 g	% calories from fat: 41%	Cholesterol: 107 mg	Sodium: 436 mg

A Few More Vegetable Ideas

Artichokes • For the outdoor grill only. Trim the artichokes, leaving 1 inch of stem, and spread the leaves as much as possible. Peel the stem. Whisk together some olive oil, garlic put through a press, lemon juice, and salt and pepper. Drizzle the dressing down into the leaves and grill the artichokes over low coals, stem side down, for about 30 minutes. Test for doneness. Cool, remove the chokes, and serve at room temperature.

Asparagus • Asparagus takes on a wonderful nutty flavor when grilled—either indoors or out. Peel the stems, coat them with olive oil, and season with salt. Grill until they're tender and the tips are slightly golden. Sprinkle with grated Parmesan. Stem shiitake mushrooms and grill them along with the asparagus. It's a dynamite combination.

Belgian Endive • Too often ignored cooked, endive takes well to grilling. Slice large heads lengthwise and drizzle them with olive oil, lemon juice, and a little sugar. Season with salt and pepper and arrange them in a basket to grill. They should be tender in about 5 minutes.

Corn on the Cob • Our favorite summer vegetable could use a little relief from the traditional lavishing of butter and salt, which carries too much guilt with the pleasure. Try this: Remove and discard the heavy outer husks. Pull back the pale ones, exposing the full ear of corn, and remove the silk. Brush the corn with half extra-virgin olive oil and half melted butter and sprinkle generously with minced fresh cilantro. Pull the soft husks back up and grill the corn over moderately hot coals for 7 to 8 minutes. You can try the same procedure with just olive oil and chili powder or snipped fresh chives. For a super treat, try sprinkling the corn with Pico de Gallo and grated Jack cheese or cheddar.

Fennel • Fennel cooks quickly on a moderately hot grill, indoors or out. Trim off the top, remove the heavy outer stalks, and cut the bulb in half. Oil it lightly and season with salt and freshly ground black pepper. Grill until it softens and chars slightly. Fennel loses its natural anise taste when cooked, so it benefits from a dusting of minced fresh tarragon before serving.

Mushrooms • Giant, meaty portobello mushrooms are ideal for grilling. Oil and season them and grill, cap side down, until you see their juices rise up through the gills. Either enjoy them as a side dish right away, or store them to add to pasta sauces or slice over grilled fish, poultry, or meat on another occasion.

Onions • Never miss a chance to grill a couple of sweet onions over a dying fire for serving another night. Just before they soften, brush them with your favorite barbecue sauce and let it caramelize and glaze the onions. Chop them before storing and pile them on top of your next hamburger or grilled chicken.

Peppers • Roasted peppers of any color or type—from sweet to fiery hot—keep quite well in the refrigerator, protected with olive oil. If you have some, don't waste a dying fire. Toss them whole on the grill and blacken them all over. Pop them in a plastic bag and when they're cool, rub the skins off with your fingers. Stem and seed them and tear them apart along their natural ribs. Put them in a small container or screw-top jar and cover them with olive oil.

Index

Metric Equivalencies

Liquid and Dry Measure Equivalencies •

CUSTOMARY	METRIC
¼ teaspoon	1.25 milliliters
½ teaspoon	2.5 milliliters
1 teaspoon	5 milliliters
1 tablespoon	15 milliliters
1 fluid ounce	30 milliliters
¼ cup	60 milliliters
⅓ cup	80 milliliters
½ cup	120 milliliters
1 cup	240 milliliters
1 pint (*2 cups*)	480 milliliters
1 quart (*4 cups; 32 ounces*)	960 milliliters (*.96 liter*)
1 gallon (*4 quarts*)	3.84 liters
1 ounce (*by weight*)	28 grams
¼ pound (*4 ounces*)	114 grams
1 pound (*16 ounces*)	454 grams
2.2 pounds	1 kilogram (*1,000 grams*)

Oven Temperature Equivalencies •

DESCRIPTION	°FAHRENHEIT	°CELSIUS
Cool	200	90
Very slow	250	120
Slow	300–325	150–160
Moderately slow	325–350	160–180
Moderate	350–375	180–190
Moderately hot	375–400	190–200
Hot	400–450	200–230
Very hot	450–500	230–260